A 90-DAY DEVOTIONAL

A
LEADER
OF
PURPOSE
AND
POWER

DR. MYLES MUNROE

WHITAKER
HOUSE

This devotional is based on material from Dr. Myles Munroe's books *The Spirit of Leadership* and *Becoming a Leader*.

A Leader of Purpose and Power:
A 90-Day Devotional

Munroe Global • P.O. Box N9583 • Nassau, Bahamas
www.munroeglobal.com • office@munroeglobal.com

ISBN: 979-8-88769-280-7 • eBook ISBN: 979-8-88769-281-4
Printed in the United States of America
© 2024 by Munroe Group of Companies Ltd.

Whitaker House • 1030 Hunt Valley Circle • New Kensington, PA 15068
www.whitakerhouse.com

Library of Congress Control Number: 2024938786

1 2 3 4 5 6 7 8 9 10 Ⱳ 30 29 28 27 26 25 24

CONTENTS

Part Three: The Spirit of Leadership

INTRODUCTION

I believe that trapped inside you is an undiscovered leader of great value to your generation!" wrote Dr. Myles Munroe.[1]

Dr. Munroe's convictions about each person's inherent calling and ability to lead were formed through both personal experience and years of researching leadership truths and principles. "I grew up in a neighborhood where there was poverty, and questionable characters were always present, exerting a negative influence," he said. But when he was a young teenager, he received a Bible and started to study its principles for life and leadership. "I began to believe what the Scriptures said rather than what I heard from outside sources, and that is how I developed a leadership mentality."

For more than thirty years, serving as the founder and president of Bahamas Faith Ministries International (BFMI), chief executive officer and chairman of the board of the International Third World Leaders Association, and president of the International Leadership Training Institute, Dr. Munroe's passion was to teach people of all backgrounds to recognize their God-given leadership capacity and to understand the principles of true leadership. He reached hundreds of millions through his various media programs and hundreds of thousands personally in his seminars, conferences, and training institutes in over seventy nations. His focus

1. The introduction and daily devotions in this book include edited excerpts from Dr. Myles Munroe's books *The Spirit of Leadership* (New Kensington, PA: Whitaker House, 2005) and *Becoming a Leader* (New Kensington, PA: Whitaker House, 2018).

was to assist people in discovering their personal sense of purpose and maximizing their untapped potential. He urged people to develop the inborn leader within them, and he taught those already in positions of leadership how to live in the fullness of their calling.

Dr. Munroe explained, "While we often think of leaders as 'out there,' we need to look within ourselves. Each one of us is a leader who can affect the people and institutions in our own spheres of influence. When we begin with ourselves, we will naturally have an effect on the lives of others." And he emphasized, "I discovered that the thinking of a leader is what separates him or her from the followers. I call this unique mental attitude the spirit of leadership."

This 90-day devotional, based on Dr. Munroe's popular books *The Spirit of Leadership* and *Becoming a Leader*, will help you identify your inherent aptitude to lead and the special qualities of the spirit of leadership. In this book, Dr. Munroe offers daily practical and biblical advice for making your personal leadership gifting come alive—whether you are just starting out on the path to leadership or have been in a leadership position for years. He presents essential principles for releasing your leadership spirit that many current leaders have yet to discover and many leadership training programs overlook. Included are twelve powerful attitudes for leadership and ten values of leaders.

Each day's devotion features insights and encouragement, a motivating thought for the day, and a Scripture reading. Since we discover the true purpose and power of leadership only in the mind of our Creator, it is essential to read His "Manual," as Dr. Munroe liked to call the Bible, for ourselves in order to clearly see the revelation of His leadership plan for our lives. Whenever we read God's Word, we should ask Him for wisdom to understand it. God's Holy Spirit is our Teacher, and we need to pray that He would illuminate the Word and give us insight.

Dr. Munroe's vision for the leadership principles presented in this devotional was that they would help meet the crucial need for genuine leaders in our families, churches, communities, cities, and nations. He desired that all people would awaken the hidden leader within them so they can develop and refine their leadership qualities and use them for the benefit of the world: "You were born to lead—settle for nothing less. Your generation and your world await your manifestation."

CALLED TO BE A LEADER

"Let us make mankind in our image, in our likeness, so that they may rule."   —Genesis 1:26

Are leaders born, made, developed, created, cultivated, or products of circumstances? Is leadership reserved only for an elite few, a specific gender, people of a particular social stratum, or those of advanced intelligence? Is leadership the prerogative of a rare breed? Is it a by-product of the superior DNA of a superrace? Or can anyone from anywhere at any time emerge as a leader? These questions have been around in some form for thousands of years.

My firm belief is that trapped inside of *every* human being is an undiscovered leader of great value to their generation.

Why should you become a leader? Because it is the calling of all people, regardless of age, gender, circumstance, or vocation. It is *your* calling. The most important foundation of leadership is self-discovery. The leader within you will come alive when you discover your purpose, your life's vision, and your potential, and when you set out to fulfill them all without compromise. People are not all the same, but they are all leaders in their own unique ways.

You can become the leader you were meant to be by recognizing that leadership is your God-given calling and by returning to His original purpose for you. Each of us was created to be a leader led by the Spirit of God. We are all inherent leaders, designed by God with the potential to lead in the image of our Creator, through the power and guidance of His Spirit.

Perhaps, lying deep within you, buried by the misconception that only special people are called to the lofty position of leader, is one of the greatest leaders of our time. If you are in doubt about your leadership capacities, it is essential that you change your concept of leadership now and see yourself the way your Creator sees you.

My purpose is to challenge your concept of the limitations of your own abilities and ignite in you the conviction that you were called to lead. As you commit to the process of becoming a leader, you will be able to do the following:

+ Discover your true self and bring meaning and fulfillment to your life

+ Develop the gifts and talents you were meant to share with the world

+ Leave a legacy that will be an influence for good long after you are gone

There is a leader in every one of us just waiting to be released. Are you ready to discover the leader within you and to fulfill your purpose and calling?

⌒

Thought: You can become the leader you were meant to be by recognizing that leadership is your God-given calling and by returning to God's original purpose for you.

Reading: Genesis 1:26–28

— Day 2 —
WHAT DISTINGUISHES TRUE LEADERS?

"For God has not given us a spirit of fear, but of power and of love and of a sound mind."   —2 Timothy 1:7 (NKJV)

In over three decades of leadership research and training others on the nature and principles of true leadership, I have been able to help many people to find their visions, renew their focus, and produce a better life. I am humbled and honored by the privilege of helping others achieve their personal and corporate goals. However, for many of those years, I still had one major challenge: I could not understand why, no matter how many principles, precepts, and programs people were taught about leadership, there always seemed to be a missing ingredient preventing many of them from breaking through to the leadership capacity I knew existed within them.

I had read hundreds of books, journals, and research papers on the subject of leadership; I had attended countless seminars, conferences, and summits dealing with leadership development, yet I was never able to identify, define, or fully understand the mystery key that separated and distinguished the leader from the follower. It was not until several years ago, during one of my leadership sessions with a group of government, religious, and corporate professionals in England, that I began to gain insight into this mystery of leadership. I took this insight back to my home in Nassau, the Bahamas, where I was able to study members of our organization and others to try to clarify the specific principles that make a leader different from followers. All my leadership teaching since that time has focused on the missing ingredient I found.

Simply put, I discovered that the *thinking* of a leader is what separates them from followers. I found that true leaders are distinguished by a *unique mental attitude* that emanates from an internalized discovery of self, which creates a strong, positive, and confident self-concept and self-worth. This mental attitude affects the entire life of the leader and controls their response to stress, crises, disappointments, failures, challenges, and danger. It gives the leader a sense of confidence, faith, and belief in possibilities. It inspires others to have hope in the face of great odds and causes the leader to cultivate a spirit of purpose, daring, passion, and conviction. I call this unique mental attitude *the spirit of leadership*.

Genuine leadership is birthed in the womb of a personal revelation within the leader and manifests itself in specific and characteristic qualities. In the following days, we will look at how a person can experience a personal revelation of leadership, and we will identify the special attitudes of this spirit.

Together, we will discover that leadership is not the result of study or ordination, position, or power. Man (humanity) is essentially a spirit-being, and the nature of a person's spirit dictates the nature that they manifest. Until a person's spirit is changed, the person is unchanged. Leadership, therefore, begins in the spirit of a person. When the spirit of leadership comes alive, it produces an attitude that separates the leader from the follower.

Every human has the instinct and capacity for leadership, but most do not have the courage or will to cultivate it. All humans possess the potential to lead, but most have lost the passion of leadership. My goal is to help you to rediscover and recover true leadership.

Thought: Every human has the instinct and capacity for leadership, but most do not have the courage or will to cultivate it.

Reading: 2 Timothy 1:6–7

—Day 3—

WHERE ARE THE TRUE LEADERS?

"I sought for a man among them, that should make up the hedge, and stand in the gap before me…: but I found none."
—Ezekiel 22:30 (kjv)

There is nothing as elusive as true leadership.

All the money in the world can make you rich, and all the power in the world can make you strong, but these things can never make you a leader. You can inherit a fortune, but you can never inherit true leadership. True leadership gives people a cause, a reason for living that gives meaning to their lives so that they feel necessary and purposeful.

Our greatest challenge today is that of a leadership vacuum. The number one need all over the globe is not money, social programs, or even new governments. It is quality, disciplined, principle-centered leadership. We need true leadership in our governments, businesses, schools, civic institutions, youth communities, religious organizations, homes, and in every arena of life. However, the search for genuine leadership is becoming increasingly difficult.

The complex, uncharted waters of the twenty-first century have plunged us into a world of globalization, terrorism, recession, famines, health epidemics, corporate and governmental compromises, religious conflicts, and cultural clashes. These conditions demand the highest quality of leadership that our generation can produce. Yet I have sat in the halls of government and corporate power and observed the struggles of today's leaders to deal with the challenges they face. Many leaders just don't know how to lead any longer. There is no greater need in our world today than effective, competent, moral leadership.

This crisis in leadership is on many people's minds. Questions about moral integrity, honor, values, role models, and respectable standards are topics of discussion on countless news programs and in the thoughts of the man on the street, all asking the same question: *Where are the true leaders today?*

Why is true leadership so difficult to find? Morals, ethics, principles, convictions, standards, faithfulness, transparency, trustworthiness, and honesty are rare commodities in the field of contemporary leadership. We are in desperate need of true, competent, principled, sensitive, compassionate, and spiritually conscious leaders.

Leadership gives each of us an outlet for expressing our own gifting, discovering a sense of significance and purpose to our generation, and making a commitment to deliver that purpose as a passion. In our journey together, we will uncover the missing ingredients in true leadership development, the elusive links between talent, titles, and leadership. We will answer these important questions: What makes a genuine leader? When does one truly become a leader? What are the specific qualities that distinguish leaders from followers?

True leadership is not a result of memorizing formulas, learning skills, imitating methods, or training in techniques. True leadership is an attitude of the heart.

Thought: Leadership gives each of us an outlet for expressing our own gifting, discovering a sense of significance and purpose, and making a commitment to deliver that purpose as a passion.

Reading: Proverbs 28:2–4

— Day 4 —
LEADERS FOR THE NATIONS

"For lack of guidance a nation falls, but victory is won through many advisers." —Proverbs 11:14

Over the last few days, we have seen that despite the inherent leadership potential in every person, very few individuals realize this power, and fewer still have responded effectively to the call. As a result, our nations, societies, and communities are suffering from an astounding leadership void.

Where are the true national leaders? Where are the leaders who are willing to take responsibility for the present situation and conditions in their individual countries? Who is willing to accept the challenge, to face it head-on with integrity, character, and a commitment to execute righteous judgment for a better world?

In every nation, our governments are being undermined because of a lack of leaders. Our homes are crying out for leadership. Our youth are begging for leaders. The church is suffering from an absence of leaders. Our communities need positive role models, our children need fathers, and our world needs direction. From America to Australia, from Croatia to the Caribbean, and from Uganda to Uruguay, the world is in desperate need of true leaders.

This is not the first time that a dearth of quality, effective leadership has been the norm throughout the world. Yet a quick glance at the historical record shows that during periods when moral, social, economic, spiritual, and political chaos have gripped nations, the greatest leaders have surfaced. Again, the answer to our problems is qualified, just, and righteous leaders. *Quality leadership* is the key to prosperous and peaceful lives and nations.

The biblical record reveals God's demand for quality leaders during times of human crisis. His search for effective leadership is expressed in numerous statements, such as these:

> *Appoint judges and officials for each of your tribes in every town the* Lord *your God is giving you, and they shall judge the people fairly. Do not pervert justice or show partiality. Do not accept a bribe, for a bribe blinds the eyes of the wise and twists the words of the innocent. Follow justice and justice alone, so that you may live and possess the land the* Lord *your God is giving you.*   (Deuteronomy 16:18–20)

> *I urge, then, first of all, that requests, prayers, intercession and thanksgiving be made for all people—for kings and all those in authority, that we may live peaceful and quiet lives in all godliness and holiness.*   (1 Timothy 2:1–2)

These and other passages of Scripture indicate that whenever a nation lacks quality, legitimate, and just leaders, nationwide deterioration occurs. However, just as it is impossible for a bitter spring to bring forth sweet water (see James 3:11–18), it is impossible for an unrighteous world to produce righteous leaders or for an unjust system to produce just characteristics. God's remedy for this type of situation is the discovery and raising up of new, trained leaders committed to justice and righteousness.

⟨⟩

Thought: God desires to raise up leaders committed to justice and righteousness.

Reading: Psalm 2:10–12

THE ULTIMATE MODEL OF LEADERSHIP

"Then [Jesus] said to them, 'Follow Me, and I will make you fishers of men.'"   —Matthew 4:19 (NKJV)

A popular definition of leadership is that "leadership is influence." It is true that influence is a defining factor in true leadership. However, I believe that this is an incomplete description because it does not distinguish *what kind* of influence or *the source* of that influence in a leader's life.

The ultimate model of effective leadership—Jesus Christ of Nazareth—inspired His chosen followers so much that they left their businesses and, for a time, their families in order to follow Him. He never threatened them or forced them to come, but He inspired them and then invited them to join Him.

Born in an obscure, forgotten town in the hills of ancient Judea; raised in a village that, according to archeological research, had only one street and eleven houses; and leaving no record of having had any formal education, Jesus introduced His vision of a new world order to simple village people who themselves were considered least on the social strata. Yet His clear sense of purpose, His commitment to the cause, and His unrelenting passion and compassion inspired twelve common local businessmen—among them, four fishermen and a tax collector—to abandon their personal dreams, private priorities, and occupations to follow Him even to death.

Even though Jesus was the Creator, He became like His creation and lived on the earth. Even though He was all-powerful, He empowered humanity. Even though He was divine, He served humanity. He was without defect, yet He embraced our imperfections and took them on Himself so that we could have the freedom and ability to become leaders in our generation. That is why Jesus Christ is the ultimate model of leadership and the true source of our leadership influence.

I wrote earlier that, for decades, I have dedicated myself to the study of leadership, and I believe leadership is more than influence alone. After thousands of hours of research and reading hundreds of books on the subject, I determined to craft my own comprehensive definition of leadership as I have come to understand it. This definition incorporates the principal ingredients and components that I believe give birth to and sustain true leadership and can be applied by anyone who desires to discover and release the hidden leader within:

> *Leadership is the capacity to influence others through inspiration motivated by a passion, generated by a vision, produced by a conviction, ignited by a purpose.*

This description reveals that leadership is not a *pursuit* of something but a *result*. Under this definition, the word *leader* is not a label that you give yourself. *Leader* is what the people whom you inspire call you because they are stirred to participate in the positive vision that you are presenting to them—whether it is the vision for a country, a company, or a cause. True leadership requires the responsibility of taking followers into the exciting unknown and creating a new reality for them.

⌐⌐

Thought: True leadership is an attitude that naturally inspires and motivates others.

Reading: Mark 1:16–20

—Day 6—

FROM ORDINARY TO EXTRAORDINARY

"Moses answered the people, 'Do not be afraid. Stand firm and you will see the deliverance the LORD will bring you today.'" —Exodus 14:13

The greatest leadership seems to surface during times of personal, social, economic, political, and spiritual conflict. History has produced a legacy of outstanding leaders who have impacted the world and furthered the development of humanity. They were both men and women, rich and poor, learned and unlearned, trained and untrained. They came from every race, color, language, and culture of the world. Many of them had no ambition to become great or renowned but were "victims" of circumstances. They did not intend to be leaders, but the demands of life ignited a sleeping spirit within them. In fact, most of the individuals who have greatly affected humanity have been simple people who were thrust into situations that called forth the hidden qualities of their characters, which subsequently inspired confidence and trust within others, or they were driven by personal, passionate goals.

Let's look again at the definition of leadership that I am proposing: *Leadership is the capacity to influence others through inspiration motivated by a passion, generated by a vision, produced by a conviction, ignited by a purpose.*

When you apply this definition of leadership to every one of the people mentioned in the devotions today and tomorrow, you begin to see a common thread that explains their leadership influence. I have interspersed examples of great leaders from both ancient and contemporary times. Each of these leaders first discovered a purpose for their lives that became a passion. Their passion inspired and influenced others who personally embraced the leaders' purposes and allowed these leaders to guide them in the specific direction of their visions, which brought about radical changes in the world.

MOSES

The historic Hebrew deliverer was given a clear sense of purpose. In his writings, he described his encounter with God in the wilderness where he was told what he had been born to accomplish: freeing his fellow Hebrews, who were slaves in Egypt, and leading them to a promised land.

Moses inspired them to have the courage to abandon their painful, but accustomed, role of being a slave labor force in Egypt. The result was that they were willing to follow him out into the desert where there was no civilization and no source of food or water. They had caught the vision for this land that Moses told them about, a *"land flowing with milk and honey"* (Numbers 14:8), and were influenced to follow him into the unknown wilderness with confidence. (See Exodus 3; 4:27–30.)

DR. MARTIN LUTHER KING JR.

Dr. Martin Luther King Jr.'s unforgettable "I Have a Dream" speech encapsulates his purpose, passion, and inspiration. A leader and symbol of American Blacks' struggle for civil rights, Dr. King helped to change both laws and hearts in the United States, leading to greater equality and freedom in the country. His purpose was the pursuit of equality, and his conviction and passion were a vision of his country in which freedom was every person's right and privilege.

Thought: Leaders are often ordinary people placed in extraordinary circumstances.

Reading: Exodus 14

—DAY 7—
LEADERS WHO CHANGED THE WORLD

"And who knows but that you have come to your royal position for such a time as this?" —Esther 4:14

Today, we continue to look at examples of leaders who illustrate our working definition of leadership: *Leadership is the capacity to influence others through inspiration motivated by a passion, generated by a vision, produced by a conviction, ignited by a purpose.*

KING DAVID

King David is one of the most fascinating and remarkable leaders in the history of the world. His lifelong purpose was a desire to serve his God, restore the honor of the Jewish nation, and strengthen his people politically and militarily. David was passionate about his purpose. Soon after he was privately anointed king when he was only a boy, he leapt to prominence by defeating the giant Goliath, a member of the Philistine army that was fighting against the Israelites. (See 1 Samuel 16:1–13; 17.) Before and after he took the throne, he inspired his people through his devotion, his faith, his loyalty, and his bravery. In response, his people loved, respected, and served him. (See, for example, 1 Samuel 18:6–7; 2 Samuel 3:30–37.) Today, millions continue to be inspired by the record of the stories and events of his life, which depict his deep sense of purpose and passion.

CORRIE TEN BOOM

Corrie ten Boom was fifty years old when the Nazis invaded her native Holland. Up to that time, she had lived an obscure life with her sister as they helped their father run his watch shop and quietly practiced their Christian faith. Confronted by the reality of the Nazis' persecution and murder of the Jews, they discovered their true purpose: preserving the lives of Jews and others by hiding them in a secret room in their home. Corrie and several of her family members were eventually turned in. Corrie's father died in prison, and she and her sister were sent to a concentration camp, where her sister died. After her release from the concentration camp, Corrie found a new purpose. Traveling around the world, she told her story and urged people to find healing and freedom through forgiveness in Jesus Christ.

NELSON MANDELA

Nelson Mandela's life purpose was the elimination of the policy of apartheid and the establishment of racial equality in South Africa. He desired the formation of a free and democratic society for all people, Black and white. His passion for this purpose led him to fight for these causes, for which he was sentenced to life in prison. Following national and international pressure, Mandela was released from prison after twenty-eight years. His passion for justice and truth transformed an entire country's outlook, government, structure, and policies.

These individuals are excellent examples of true leaders whose passionate pursuit of their purposes and convictions inspired others to follow them in their vision. Our world today is in desperate need of such individuals.

〜

Thought: The greatest leadership seems to surface during times of personal, social, economic, political, and spiritual conflict.

Reading: Esther 7

—DAY 8—

THE HIDDEN LEADER WITHIN

"Then [God] said, 'I am the God of your father...' At this, Moses hid his face, because he was afraid to look at God."
—Exodus 3:6

The key to the effectiveness of the leaders we have considered over the last two days, and countless others like them not mentioned, is that they discovered the hidden leader within.

An army of sheep *led by a lion* will always defeat an army of lions *led by a sheep*. This unusual statement captures the heart of true leadership. This concept became real to me during one of my trips to the cradle of civilization, the continent of Africa. It was there, deep in the village lands of the African bush, that I heard a story that encapsulated what I believe is the missing ingredient for many people in the leadership development process.

I had just finished speaking to five thousand men and women at a leadership conference in the modern city of Harare, the capital of Zimbabwe. One of the organizers approached me and asked if I would travel to a village to speak to a group who wanted to learn more about leadership. I gladly consented, and arrangements were made for my driver—who also served as my interpreter—and me to leave at first light the next morning. We traveled for several hours along bumpy, unpaved roads, past dusty villages, and through dense green forests and jungle. When we reached our destination, I was invited into a grass-roofed building in which over three hundred men and women sat eagerly waiting for us to begin the session. It was a joy to be so well received.

Afterward, the chief of the village invited me to a special dinner, during which he told me a story that taught me a lesson in leadership I will never forget. The chief began in this way:

There was once a farmer who lived in this village and who was also a herder of sheep. One day, he took his sheep out to pasture, and while they were grazing, he heard a strange noise, which first sounded like a kitten, coming from a patch of grass. Led by his curiosity, the old shepherd went to discover the source of this insistent sound, and, to his surprise, he found a lone, shivering lion cub, obviously separated from his family. His first thought was the danger he would be in if he stayed too close to the cub. So, the old man quickly left the area and watched from a distance. When night fell, the shepherd decided that, for the survival of the lion cub, he would take him to his farmhouse and care for him.

The shepherd hand-fed this cub with fresh milk and kept him warm, safe, and secure in the protective confines of the farmhouse. The lion cub grew with the sheep and became a part of the herd. They accepted him as one of their own, and he acted like one of them. After fifteen months had passed, the little cub had become an adolescent lion, but he acted, sounded, responded, and behaved just like one of the sheep. In essence, the lion had become a sheep by association. He had lost himself and become one of them.

The young lion was no longer who he was designed to be. We will learn the rest of his story tomorrow.

⌒

Thought: Hidden within every follower is an undiscovered leader.

Reading: Exodus 3:1–10

— DAY 9 —

DISCOVERING YOUR TRUE SELF

"But Moses said to God, 'Who am I that I should go to Pharaoh and bring the Israelites out of Egypt?' And God said, 'I will be with you.'" —Exodus 3:11–12

Today, we continue the account of the young lion who was raised with sheep:

One hot day, four years later, the shepherd watched over his flock as they waded into the quiet, flowing water of a river to drink. The lion who thought he was a sheep followed them into the water. Suddenly, just across the river, there appeared out of the thick jungle bush a large beast that the lion had never seen before. The sheep panicked, leaped out of the water, and dashed toward the farm, not stopping until they were all safely huddled behind the pen. Strangely, the young lion, who was now fully grown, ran and huddled with them, stricken with fear, as the beast let out a roar that shook the forest.

Several days later, while the flock grazed, the young lion walked down to the river to drink. As he bent over the water, he suddenly panicked and ran wildly toward the farmhouse for safety, even though the sheep didn't follow him. Puzzled, the young lion walked slowly back to the water. Once more, as he drank, he saw what appeared to be the beast and froze in panic. It was his own reflection in the water.

At that moment, the beast appeared out of the jungle again. The flock dashed with breakneck speed toward the farmhouse, but before the young lion could move, the beast stepped in the water toward him and made another deafening roar that filled the forest. As fear gripped the young lion, he decided to try to appease the beast and make the same sound. At first, the only noise that came from his gaping jaws was the sound of a sheep. After several attempts, the young lion heard himself roar like the beast. He also felt stirrings in his body and feelings that he had never known before. It was as if he was experiencing a deep transformation in mind, body, and spirit.

There, in the river of life, stood two beasts growling at and to each other. As the roars filled the forest for miles around, the big beast stopped, turned his back on the young lion, and started toward the forest. Then he paused, looked at the young lion, and growled, as if to say, "Are you coming?" The young lion knew what the gesture meant and realized that his day of decision had arrived—the day he would have to choose whether to continue to live life as a sheep or to be the new self he had just discovered. He knew that, to become his true self, he would have to give up the safe, secure, predictable, and simple life of the farm and enter the frightening, wild, unpredictable, dangerous life of the jungle. It was a day to become true to himself and leave the false image of another life behind. It was an invitation to a "sheep" to become the king of the jungle. Most importantly, it was an invitation for the body of a lion to possess the spirit of a lion.

After looking back and forth at the farm and the jungle a few times, the young lion turned his back on the farm and the sheep with whom he had lived for years, and he followed the beast into the forest to become who he always had been—a lion king.

⌒

Thought: Though we are called to be leaders, we cannot *become* leaders unless we know what a leader is and understand the nature of true leadership.

Reading: Exodus 3:11–26

— DAY 10 —

A CHANGE OF HEART

"I will give you a new heart and put a new spirit in you."
—Ezekiel 36:26

Over the last two days, I related the story of the lion living among the sheep. When I first heard the village chief give this fantastic narrative, I was overcome by the deep principles it communicated relating to leaders, leadership, and the critical process involved in discovering and becoming one's true self. I went away from that encounter with a deeper understanding of why it is so difficult for many individuals to make the transition "across the river" to their true selves. I suddenly understood that lasting change could occur only when it took place in the "spirit of the mind," or mindset. Without this metamorphosis, no amount of training, study, or education could transform a follower into a leader. In essence, a converted attitude is the key to a transformed life. Until this attitude change happens, the lion will still think, act, respond, and live like a sheep instead of living like the king of the jungle.

This is why *the beginning of leadership is discovering your true self.*

Just as the young lion's newly discovered growl revealed his inherent strength, you can release the inherent leadership strength within you when you come to understand your true self. Just as the young lion watched the beast walking away and knew that he had to make a decision about his future, you have a choice to make about your own future.

Just as the young lion looked back at the farm where the sheep were and then looked toward the forest where the lion was heading, you must evaluate your past and your potential and step toward one or the other. Just as the young lion knew that, to become his true self, he would have to give up the safe, secure, predictable, and simple life of the farm and enter the frightening, wild, unpredictable, dangerous life of the jungle, you will have to leave the safe confines of being only a follower if you are going to become the leader God designed you to be.

Just as the young lion was challenged to turn his back on the farm, cross the river, and walk into the forest—leaving behind his old life as a sheep and embarking on the life he was born to live—so these devotions are designed to challenge you to cross your own river of intimidation and fear and enter the forest of true leadership, which you were created to manifest.

As one who has had to cross that river myself, my desire is to be a catalyst, like the forest beast, roaring an invitation into your life and heart and helping you to enter the adventure of discovering and releasing *the leadership spirit within you.*

⌒

Thought: A converted attitude is the key to a transformed life.

Reading: Ezekiel 36:26–27

— DAY 11 —

GENUINE LEADERSHIP GOES BEYOND

"When the righteous are in authority and become great, the people rejoice; but when the wicked man rules, the people groan and sigh." —Proverbs 29:2 (AMP)

There are many people who confuse the *position* of leadership with the *disposition* of true leadership. No matter what position one may be given, status in an organization does not automatically create leadership. Genuine leadership is one's internal disposition that relates to a sense of purpose, self-worth, and self-concept.

Some have confused leadership with the ability to control others through manipulating their emotions and playing on their fears and needs. But true leadership is a product of inspiration, not manipulation. Then there are those who believe that the title makes the leader. However, we have all seen people who have been placed in prominent positions with impressive titles yet have failed miserably because they haven't understood that real leadership is manifested in performance and results and not just in labels.

Genuine leadership goes far beyond the mechanics of most of the approaches that pervade our leadership programs today. As we have been discussing, true leadership has more to do with discovering a sense of meaning and significance in life. This distinction separates the leadership quality of passion from the hunger or lust for power. True leaders do not seek power but are driven by a passion to achieve a noble cause.

I am convinced that you were created to be a successful leader. Every human being was created to lead in an area of gifting. You were never created to be oppressed, subjugated, subordinated, or depressed. The Creator designed each human being to fulfill a specific purpose and assignment in life. Assignment determines *area* or *domain* of leadership. Deep inside each of us is a spirit with a big dream struggling to free itself from the limitations of our past experiences, present circumstances, and self-imposed doubts.

We are all victims of unfulfilled passions. I believe that man's greatest ignorance is of himself. What you believe about yourself creates your world. No human can live beyond the limits of their beliefs. In essence, you are what you believe. Your thoughts create your beliefs, your beliefs create your convictions, your convictions create your attitude, your attitude controls your perception, and your perception dictates your behavior. The result is that your life is what you *think* it should be. When you gain an understanding of how your mindset affects your life and your leadership potential, you begin the process of becoming a leader. This is the heart of true leadership: your attitude, your mindset, your "spirit of the mind."

Some of the unique attitudes or qualities of leaders include passion, initiative, teamwork, innovation, persistence, discipline, focus, time management, confidence, a positive disposition, patience, peace, and compassion. In the coming days, we will explore many of these leadership attitudes so that you can renew the spirit of your mind according to them and discover how to cultivate them in your life.

⌒

Thought: True leaders do not seek power but are driven by a passion to achieve a noble cause.

Reading: Proverbs 29:2–8

—Day 12—

CHALLENGING LEADERSHIP MYTHS

"Pride goes before destruction, a haughty spirit before a fall."
—Proverbs 16:18

As we continue to discover the nature of true leadership, let's consider the modern theories articulated by leadership "gurus" today. These theories have produced myths that should be examined and challenged. They can be summarized as follows:

Myth #1: Birth trait theory: "Leaders are born, not made." This theory is the belief that leadership is a result of special birth traits inherent in the personality and nature of the individual. It implies that some humans are born with unique qualities that earmark them for leadership, while the majority, who do not possess these traits, are destined to be led.

This concept leads us to deify our leaders as men and women who are essentially unlike us and therefore superior to us. It results in our blocking our own leadership potential and development and surrendering our untapped leadership capacity to the control and limitations of others.

Myth #2: Leadership by providence. There is a belief that certain people are chosen by "the gods" and appointed to the elite position of leadership over the unfortunate masses. In essence, leadership is reserved for the few chosen by a divine power to control, manage, and direct the life, future, fortunes, and aspirations of the un-chosen.

Myth #3: Leadership is the result of a charismatic personality. This is the theory that only certain individuals who possess a unique measure of charisma; who exhibit special traits, such as a force of will; who are extroverts; who are magnetic speakers, and so on, are leaders. The difficulty with this theory is that, in every generation, significant leaders arise who do not display the charismatic traits celebrated by this philosophy. In many cases, leaders emerge from the unique circumstances of the times in which they live without manifesting any special charisma.

Myth #4: Leadership is the product of a forceful personality. This theory emerges from the belief that leadership is the result of an authoritarian, coldly calculating, no-nonsense, hard-driving, impatient, quick-tempered, and moody personality. This false perception comes from the idea that people are fundamentally incompetent and naturally lazy and must be forced, threatened, and manipulated by their leaders and managers if anything is going to be accomplished. However, the evidence has always defied this belief, revealing that people are most productive and cooperative when they are inspired rather than manipulated by leadership.

Myth #5: Leadership is the result of special training. This is the belief that leaders are produced through special educational courses and training. Many people feel that they must have an MBA or attend leadership conferences in order to be able to lead others. There's nothing wrong with such training, in itself. Yet true leadership is not a technique, a method, a style, or the acquisition of skills. As we have discovered, it is the manifestation of an attitude based on the knowledge of who you were born to be.

Ask yourself if you have accepted of any of these myths. If so, they may be holding you back from the leadership you are called to. Remember that your attitude about yourself has a tremendous impact on your daily life and whether you fulfill your central life purpose.

⌒

Thought: Modern theories of leadership have produced myths that must be examined and challenged.

Reading: Proverbs 16:18–23

— Day 13 —

THE ESSENCE OF THE HUMAN SPIRIT

"But it is the spirit in a person, the breath of the Almighty, that gives them understanding." —Job 32:8

Through my study of the foundational truths of leadership, I have discovered two distinct aspects of leaders that I would like us to explore together so that you can better understand your leadership potential and the attitude that accompanies it. In order to reach your destiny, it is vital that you comprehend both aspects.

The first is what I call the *leadership spirit*, which is the *inherent leadership nature* bestowed on all of humanity by the Creator. In the days to come, we will spend significant time uncovering the origin and nature of our God-given leadership spirit.

Later, we will look closely at the second distinct aspect of leaders—what I call the *spirit of leadership*—which encompasses the crucial *attitudes* and *mindset* we must have to ignite the leadership spirit within us and to live out our divinely appointed leadership potential. But for now, we will focus on the *leadership spirit*.

Earlier, I stated my belief that "trapped in every follower is a hidden leader." If this is the case, we may ask, "Where did this inherent leadership potential come from? And if it exists, why do so many people never seem to exhibit it or show some evidence of its presence?" These questions point to the heart of this teaching on the *leadership spirit*.

To understand this concept and its underlying principle, it is necessary for us to go back to the very beginning: creation. Our journey takes us back to the beginning so we may uncover the principles inherent in the nature of creation. Leadership is not something that human beings need to strive for; it is something that we already have been given because of the Creator's purpose and design for us.

My personal definition of the leadership spirit is the following:

The inherent capacity of the human spirit to lead, manage, and dominate, which was placed there at the point of creation and made necessary by the purpose and assignment for which man (both male and female) was created.

The leadership spirit was given by God to humanity and is the essence of our human spirit. In effect, man doesn't *have* a spirit; man *is* a spirit, and that spirit is an expression of God's Spirit. The essential nature of His Spirit is in our spirits because He is the Source from which we come. Leadership is really a discovery of who we truly are in God's design and the application of that discovery to our lives. Simply put, true leadership is *self-discovery* and *self-manifestation.*

Recognizing the leadership spirit is key to understanding ourselves. Men and women don't actually *become* leaders, as if leadership were an option among other choices. Rather, when we realize God's design for us in creation and become our true selves, we will naturally *be* leaders. We will desire to maximize all our gifts and talents in the fulfillment of our purposes in life. In order to understand this critical point, we will continue to examine all the aspects of the leadership spirit.

Thought: The leadership spirit is the essence of the spirit-man, who can comprehend his identity only from relating to his Source.

Reading: Job 32:6–9

—Day 14—

THE CREATOR'S PURPOSE

"In the beginning God created the heavens and the earth."
—Genesis 1:1

I have discovered that people's concepts of the origin of life clearly influence the way they think about themselves, including their ideas about their leadership potential. Some believe that their existence is the random result of evolution, so that there is no specific purpose for life—it exists merely as a result of forces of nature. This theory also supports the idea that those who are stronger—physically, intellectually, or creatively—are destined to lead and control others, while the rest are destined to be followers. Other people understand that we were created by an eternal Creator who had a purpose and plan for humanity from the beginning of time. This concept supports the idea that every person has a role and contribution to make, no matter their station in life and current level of ability.

Certain principles found in the book of Genesis changed my life by enabling me to better comprehend the very nature of life itself. The biblical record tells us that, in the beginning, God created the heavens and the earth and fashioned everything to sustain life. From the following verses in Genesis 1, we notice that everything that lives on the earth was somehow sourced by the earth and thus consists of the earth's elements:

> *Then God said, "Let the land produce vegetation: seed-bearing plants and trees on the land that bear fruit with seed in it, according to their various kinds." And it was so.... And God saw that it was good.* (verses 11–12)

And God said, "Let the water teem with living creatures, and let birds fly above the earth across the vault of the sky." So God created the great creatures of the sea and every living thing with which the water teems and moves about in it, according to their kinds, and every winged bird according to its kind. And God saw that it was good. (verse 20–21)

And God said, "Let the land produce living creatures according to their kinds: the livestock, the creatures that move along the ground, and the wild animals, each according to its kind." And it was so.... And God saw that it was good. (verse 24–25)

Vegetation, birds, and animals, in essence, came from the soil. Fish and other sea creatures were created from the waters, and the stars were produced out of the firmament (see verses 14–18). All the wonderful products of creation that we have on and near earth consist of whatever their source is, and when they die, they, in effect, return to the components of that source.

The important precepts hidden in these creative acts may be summarized in the following principles: (1) God first established the purpose of whatever He desired to make. (2) God identified the material from which each product in creation was to be made. (3) God directed His creative speech to the material from which He desired the product to be made. (4) The product possessed the same components as the source from which it was derived, and therefore possessed the same potential. Thus, the principle "source determines resource" is applicable to all that God created—including humanity.

⌒

Thought: God first established the purpose of whatever He desired to make.

Reading: Genesis 1

—Day 15—

"LET US MAKE MAN"

*"So God created mankind in his own image, in the image of
God he created them."*   —Genesis 1:27

When God made the vegetation, animals, sea creatures, and
stars, He directed His creative speech to the soil, the water, and
the firmament. But when it came to creating the human species,
God's focus changed.

> *Then God said, "Let Us make man in Our image, according
> to Our likeness; let them have dominion over the fish of the sea,
> over the birds of the air, and over the cattle, over all the earth
> and over every creeping thing that creeps on the earth."*
>
> (Genesis 1:26 NKJV)

The most amazing distinction here is that, in His creation of
mankind, God did not speak to earthly things—the soil, the water,
or the firmament. He spoke to *Himself,* saying, *"Let Us make man
in Our image, in Our likeness."* Many of us miss the essential point
here. Humans were not just *made* by God; they were intentionally
drawn out of *His own nature.* The word *"image"* used in this verse
means the following in the original Hebrew text:

> *selem* (6754), "statue; image; copy."... The word...means
> "image" in the sense of essential nature.... Human nature
> in its internal and external characteristics.... So, too, God
> made man in His own "image," reflecting some of His
> own perfections: perfect in knowledge, righteousness, and
> holiness, and with dominion over the creatures.... In Gen.
> 1:26 (the first occurrence of the word) the "image" of God

is represented by two Hebrew words (*selem* and *demut*)."[2]

The word for "*likeness*" in Genesis 1:26 is similar to the one for "*image*" but embraces an additional meaning: "*demut* (1823), 'likeness; shape; figure; form; pattern.'.... First, the word means 'pattern,' in the sense of the specifications from which an actual item is made."[3] The verb form of *likeness* is the following: "*damah* (1819), 'to be like, resemble, be or act like, liken or compare, devise, balance or ponder.'"[4]

Why is it so important to understand these words and their implications? Because these are the words that define and describe the essence of your composition, capacity, ability, potential, and value as a human being. They also confirm and reveal how God designed you and why.

According to these definitions, to be made in God's image and likeness means that you possess the spiritual nature, characteristics, and "substances" of God and are a reflection of His spiritual qualities. It also denotes that you were designed to be like, act like, and function like the Creator. In essence, God created you from His own substance and released you from His own Spirit. The reason He did this is the key to understanding the nature of the human leadership spirit. It is the reason why we look to Him as the divine *Source* of our inherent ability to be leaders. It all has to do with the *purpose* for which God made us.

⌇

Thought: Humans were not just made by God but drawn out of His own nature.

Reading: Genesis 1:26–31

2. W. E. Vine, Merrill F. Unger, and William White Jr., eds., *Vine's Complete Expository Dictionary of Old and New Testament Words* (Nashville: Thomas Nelson Publishers, 1996), 244.
3. *Vine's*, 136.
4. *Vine's*, 136.

—DAY 16—
WHAT IS OUR SOURCE?

"[Jesus] *is before all things, and in him all things hold together.*"   —Colossians 1:17

Years ago, I was a student at a renowned university, and one of my areas of study was fine art. In this course, we had to produce paintings, stone sculptures, drawings, and other artwork in a variety of media. I loved the stone and wood sculpture work, but, more importantly, I learned a significant lesson concerning the principles of source and resource and their relation to man's inherent purpose and potential. This lesson has cultivated and formed the foundation of my understanding of leadership and my philosophy of life itself.

On two occasions, I set about working on a wood and stone sculpture project and chose my raw material from discarded pieces of tree and stone. After laboring many hours following the design I had developed, the day came when I was finally finished with the two sculptures and was proud of the results. When I submitted my project to the professor, I obtained an A and was successful in fulfilling my requirements for graduation. I was so proud of my sculptures that I took them home with me and placed them in a very prominent place in my apartment.

A year later, however, something happened that changed the life of my sculptures forever. I decided to clean the wooden sculpture and wax the stonework. As I picked up the wooden piece to shine the results of my hard work, part of the wood stayed on the table and the other part came off in my hands. My heart sank as the bottom of the figure then gave way and fell apart right before my eyes.

Deeply shocked at this turn of events, I moved to the stone sculpture and wondered if the same thing would happen. As I rubbed it lightly with the cloth, the stone began to come apart like dust. With great disappointment, I had to accept the reality that all my work had been in vain and that the rest of my artwork was destined for disintegration. Today, both pieces are only memories, but I cherish the lesson this experience taught me. Here is the great wisdom I gained from the wood and stone sculptures:

1. The nature of the composition of *the source material* determines the nature of the composition of *the product* made or produced from it.

2. Whatever is in the source is in the product.

3. The strength and durability of the source determines the durability of the product made from it.

4. The key principle is that a thing consists of the same components and consistency as that from which it came.

5. In other words (as we saw in the account of creation): *Source determines resource.*

We must ask ourselves, "What or whom am I looking to as the source for my life?"

⌇

Thought: The strength and durability of the source determines the durability of the product made from it.

Reading: Colossians 1:15–18

— Day 17 —

CREATED TO HAVE DOMINION

"For everything comes from him and exists by his power and is intended for his glory. All glory to him forever!"
—Romans 11:36 (NLT)

Since God poured out His own nature into human beings when He created us, He is the Source and the significance of our leadership spirit. In this sense, as humans, we are a distinct portion of the "poured-out" God. Our creation in God's image is the foundational proof that you and I were created to lead. Leadership is inherent in our nature and is fundamental to our origins, our human makeup—and our destiny.

Today, we will explore some further implications of the truths revealed in Genesis 1 that we have been reviewing in this devotional.

God created us in His *image* and *likeness*. These words connote His authority, His character, and His moral and spiritual nature. Power and rulership are part of God's nature. He is the King and Ruler of the universe. Therefore, since man was made in God's image, deeply embedded in the nature of man is the spirit of rulership and authority. In the parallel creation account in the second chapter of Genesis, we read that the Creator *breathed His own life into human beings* (see Genesis 2:7), further imparting His own nature to them.

God established the role and function of human beings in relationship to the earth by stating, *"Let them have dominion...over all the earth"* (Genesis 1:26 NKJV). It is critical for us to understand the word *"dominion,"* for this is God's expressed purpose for the creation of mankind. The Hebrew term translated *"dominion"* is *radah*, which means "to tread down, i.e. subjugate; spec. to crumble off:—(come to, make to) have dominion, prevail against, reign, (bear, make to) rule."[5] Mankind was created to have dominion—it was and is God's mandate for humanity.

> *So God created mankind in his own image, in the image of God he created them; male and female he created them. God blessed them and said to them, "Be fruitful and increase in number; fill the earth and subdue it. Rule over the fish in the sea and the birds in the sky and over every living creature that moves on the ground."* (Genesis 1:27–28)

The above declaration confirms God's ordination of the following principles: (1) God created man to rule, or to have dominion, over the earth. (2) Human beings are meant to rule according to God's nature and Spirit. (3) God gave dominion over the earth to both male and female to dominate, not to be dominated. (4) God never gave people the authority to dominate one another. (For example, the male is not to dominate the female, and vice versa. People of one nation are not to dominate those of another.)

God created all of us to rule, govern, control, and influence the earth in conjunction with all other human beings. He created each of us to lead. Humanity's rulership over the earth includes the concepts of cultivating and protecting it as its stewards. These ideas all reflect the concept of leadership, which can be fulfilled in a variety of contexts and describes God's purpose for our lives.

Thought: God created us to rule, govern, control, and influence the earth in conjunction with all other human beings.

Reading: Romans 11:33–36

---

5. *Strong's Exhaustive Concordance of the Bible,* #H7287.

— DAY 18 —
THE CREATOR IS A LEADER-MAKER

"Before I formed you in the womb I knew you, before you were born I set you apart; I appointed you as a prophet to the nations." —Jeremiah 1:5

The Creator is a leader-maker. Being made in the image and likeness of God means that we were ordained by Him to be leaders. He did not produce us and then decide that He would develop us into leaders. We were designed with that in mind. I'm convinced that people's desire for power over others is a distortion of something good—it's a distortion of their inherent human desire to exercise leadership dominion.

Since each of us was created to rule, govern, control, master, manage, and lead our environments, it is my firm belief that the nature of each human being is to be in control of his environment and circumstances. You are in essence a leader, no matter who you are, regardless of whether you manifest it or not. Whether you are rich, poor, young, old, male, female, black, white, a citizen of an industrialized nation, a citizen of a third-world nation, educated, or uneducated—you have the nature and capacity for leadership. Yet you can fulfill your inherent leadership potential only when you discover, understand, develop, and begin to exercise who you are designed to be and the nature of your true leadership potential.

It doesn't matter whether you are the CEO of a large corporation, a teacher, a homemaker, the owner of a small business, a construction worker, an artist, a clerk, a government worker, a farmer, a student, a doctor, or any other vocation or position in life: the self-discovery of your inherent leadership potential and an understanding of who you are and what you are meant to be are the keys to fulfilling your purpose for existence as a leader.

The unique attitudes of leaders that distinguish them from followers produce certain behaviors that stretch them beyond the limitations of the norm. Therefore, if you are currently only in the position of a follower, this doesn't negate your inherent leadership potential. Knowing and cultivating certain attitudes about yourself will give you the mindset you need to develop your leadership potential to the fullest and fulfill what you were born to do.

Throughout this devotional, we will continue to address the qualities and characteristics of the spirit of leadership—the unique attitudes that all true leaders possess—and the fact that you can cultivate and develop them. These attitudes are necessary if you are to experience the manifestation of your leadership capacity. They can be learned, developed, and refined through practice and the exercise of responsibility. When they come together in your life, then you will fulfill the definition of a leader: you will have *the capacity to influence others through inspiration motivated by a passion, generated by a vision, produced by a conviction, ignited by a purpose.*

Each day, remind yourself that human beings were created to be leaders and were designed with the ability to manifest their leadership nature. The past and future of mankind is leadership. Leadership is your destiny.

Thought: The unique attitudes of leaders that distinguish them from followers produce certain behaviors that stretch them beyond the limitations of the norm.

Reading: Jeremiah 1:4–9

— Day 19 —

LEADERSHIP IS A PROCESS

"In their hearts humans plan their course, but the Lord *establishes their steps."*
                                            —Proverbs 16:9

Let's review once more our working definition of leadership: *the capacity to influence others through inspiration motivated by a passion, generated by a vision, produced by a conviction, ignited by a purpose.*

This definition presents leadership as the product of a *process* and not as a specific objective to pursue. It is an important distinction. In other words, there is a process we can follow to reach a position of genuine leadership. For one to *become* a leader, the process of leadership must begin at the foundation—which is the discovery of a *personal sense of meaning and purpose.* That is the first step, and it is at the very heart of leadership.

If you are going to be an effective leader, you must prepare yourself by entering into this process and being transformed by it. The following is the progression of leadership development, each element of which is indispensable:

Purpose→Conviction→Vision→Passion→

Inspiration→Influence→Leadership

- *Purpose* leads a person to develop a deep *conviction* about their obligation to humanity and to the life God has given them.

- *Conviction* emerges as a conceptual view of the future they desire, which is called a *vision.*

- *Vision* leads to the development of specific plans to accomplish their purpose, and it stirs a deep *passion* within them.

- *Passion* explodes in the individual's intense desire to accomplish their purpose, and it *inspires* all who come into their presence.

- *Inspiration* occurs when the person's expression of their inner passion resonates deeply with other people, *influencing* them to join the pursuit of the vision.

- *Influence*, the ultimate effect of inspiration, results in followers acknowledging the individual as a *leader*.

True leadership is impossible unless all these ingredients are present and integrated as a whole, producing a force for change in communities, societies, and the world. A leader is one whose internal disposition relates to a sense of purpose, self-worth, and vision for the benefit of mankind. This is leadership without limitations, in the sense that the leaders believe they can do anything necessary to fulfill their purposes. Once that process occurs, a leader becomes unstoppable.

A general concept of leadership, therefore, includes the capacity to *influence, inspire, direct, encourage, motivate, induce, move, mobilize*, and *activate* others to pursue a common purpose, interest, or goal while maintaining *commitment, momentum, confidence*, and *courage*. By its very nature, leadership incorporates an individual purpose and vision that provide the fuel for inspiration, motivation, and mobilization.

Up to this point, have you thought of leadership as a *process?* Consider this: Which elements of the process (purpose, conviction, vision, passion, inspiration, and influence) are a distinct part of your leadership journey today? How might you cultivate them?

⌐⌐

Thought: If you are going to be an effective leader, you must prepare yourself by entering into the process of leadership development and being transformed by it.

Reading: Jeremiah 29:11–13

THE POWER OF PURPOSE

"The plans of the LORD stand firm forever, the purposes of his heart through all generations."　　　　　—Psalm 33:11

We were created to be like God and to act and function as He does. God's nature includes His characteristics: He is love. He is just. He is holy. He is kind. He is patient. He is also purposeful: *"The plans of the LORD stand firm forever, the purposes of his heart through all generations"* (Psalm 33:11). His purposes are reflected in some of His titles, such as King of the universe and Father to His people.

To capture your meaning and purpose in life, you must apply the nature and purposes of God as you lead in His image on earth. His nature and our nature, and His purpose and our purposes, are meant to be intimately tied together. Remember, our purpose isn't about us—it's about our Creator. It is about what He wants us to be and do to reflect His nature and fulfill His plans for the world. His purpose was established well before we had any plans for our lives. We are meant to consult God to find out His purposes for us so we can make the right plans.

Since the Creator's purpose for our existence is leadership, management, and dominion over the earthly realm, we must clearly understand these principles of purpose as they relate to creation:

1. Purpose determines design.

2. Purpose determines potential and capacity.

3. Purpose determines natural talents.

4. Purpose determines natural desires.

5. Purpose determines fulfillment and personal satisfaction.

6. Purpose is the source of passion.

7. Purpose gives meaning to existence.

8. Purpose is the measure of success and failure.

Through these statements about purpose, we are led to this vital principle: *If something is created to do something, it is designed with the ability to do it.* This concept is at the heart of the leadership spirit. If we were created to be leaders, then each one of us must possess the capacity, inherent desire, natural talents, potential, and abilities that correspond to being a leader. You cannot demand from a product what it does not have.

Recall what God required of humanity. The Creator expressed His intent and assignment for human beings through what He said they were to do. God wasn't speaking just to the first man, Adam, but to all humanity, because inside that one man were the seeds of all mankind. The Creator's intent was that humans rule and dominate both *with* Him and *for* Him. His purpose from the beginning was to share His rulership and His administration of creation with humanity—with you and me.

‿͡)

Thought: Your purpose in life is reflected in the purpose of the Creator.

Reading: Romans 8:28–30

— Day 21 —
DISCOVERING YOUR UNIQUE PURPOSE

"For we are God's handiwork, created in Christ Jesus to do good works, which God prepared in advance for us to do."
—Ephesians 2:10

How do you discover your unique purpose—your personal "divine deposit of destiny"?

God created each person with a distinct design. He created us with unique and inherent gifts, abilities, and talents that increase our leadership effectiveness. We can begin to discover our purpose by looking inside ourselves to see what He has placed within us.

Ask yourself, "What is my dream?" and "What is my gifting?" What you are gifted in often reveals the type of leadership you are meant to exercise and the domain you are to operate in. You can also think about these questions: "What do I imagine myself doing?" "Do I have persistent thoughts about accomplishing something specific?" "What problem do I feel compelled to solve?" Answering questions such as these is vital for discovering your God-given purpose. Once you know your purpose, you can evaluate your natural gifts and abilities to see how they will help you to fulfill it.

Remember, God has given every person a unique purpose in life. My own purpose is the transformation of followers into leaders and leaders into agents of change, as well as the maximization of individual potential. The endeavors I am involved in—writing books, teaching, mentoring, training, consulting, broadcasting—all relate to, and are an expression of, that specific purpose.

Again, each person is a leader regarding their own purpose and domain of influence. One individual's purpose might lead to a calling in teaching, while another's purpose might be fulfilled in aerospace engineering or artistic endeavors. The possibilities are endless. Moreover, purposes are not always realized in conventional careers or pursuits but in a wide variety of endeavors and in personal character traits that impact the lives of others for good, such as the influence of parents on a child. A person's purpose may be fulfilled in various ways and spheres.

In essence, to enable each human being to have dominion in their own domain, the Creator has given every one of us a unique makeup and identity. This coincides with His purposes for us, which He redeemed through the work of Jesus Christ: *"For we are God's handiwork, created in Christ Jesus to do good works, which God prepared in advance for us to do"* (Ephesians 2:10). God planned in advance all that you were created to be and accomplish. When you seek His purposes, you will begin to discover the *"good works"* that you were born to do.

Whatever domain God has called you to, there is a great need for your leadership. We may never know in our lifetimes the full impact of our influence and actions, large or small. If you do not discover your personal leadership potential, you will not be able to fulfill your life's assignment. You will deprive your generation and future generations of your unique and important contribution to the world. In light of this truth, developing one's leadership potential should not be optional for anyone. We have a responsibility to find, perform, and complete our purposes.

⌣⌐

Thought: God has given each one of us a purpose in order to accomplish something in our generation.

Reading: Psalm 33:11–15

— DAY 22 —

PURPOSE REDIRECTS LIFE

"God, who set me apart from my mother's womb and called me by his grace, was pleased to reveal his Son in me so that I might preach him among the Gentiles."

—Galatians 1:15–16

An excellent example of self-discovery and purpose from the biblical record is the life of theologian Paul of Tarsus. We find his story, written by the physician Luke, in chapters seven through twenty-two of the book of Acts. As a young Pharisee, Paul (then called Saul) thought he was fulfilling his purpose in life by hunting down and killing Christians—men and women who had been reconciled to the Creator through Jesus Christ.

Saul began to destroy the church. Going from house to house, he dragged off both men and women and put them in prison.

(Acts 8:3)

Meanwhile, Saul was still breathing out murderous threats against the Lord's disciples. He went to the high priest and asked him for letters to the synagogues in Damascus, so that if he found any there who belonged to the Way, whether men or women, he might take them as prisoners to Jerusalem.

(Acts 9:1–2)

As a result of his intense hatred of Christians, Saul was filled with rage and vengeance. He was tearing down rather than building up.

Fortunately, when Jesus intervened to stop him, Saul's reconciliation with God led to the revelation of his own unique *life purpose.* (See Acts 9:15–16.) The natural qualities Saul possessed—passion, energy, and perseverance—were then put to use in the positive purpose for which God had called him. Paul later wrote this about his purpose: "*God, who set me apart from my mother's womb and called me by his grace, was pleased to reveal his Son in me so that I might preach him among the Gentiles*" (Galatians 1:15–16).

In a remarkable turnaround, Saul, whose name was changed to Paul to reflect his newfound purpose, became an instrument of reconciliation rather than an instrument of destruction. His wholehearted relationship with God and his keen intellect led to his becoming the greatest theologian the world has ever known. His Spirit-inspired writings comprise approximately one-third of the New Testament. Paul discovered his leadership purpose.

Let me emphasize once again that although you were *born to lead*, you must *become* a leader. One of my favorite quotes on leadership was written by Professor Warren Bennis: "The point is to become yourself, to use yourself completely—all your skills, gifts, and energies—in order to make your vision manifest."[6] This full expression of yourself as God created you brings Him glory and allows your vision to come to fruition. It is in this light that everyone can become a leader.

Thought: God created you as someone special and original. Discover yourself and become a leader.

Reading: Acts 9:1–31

---

6. Warren G. Bennis, *On Becoming a Leader* (New York: Basic Books, 2003), 104.

THE POWER OF CONVICTION

"Have I not commanded you? Be strong and courageous. Do not be afraid; do not be discouraged, for the LORD your God will be with you wherever you go."   —Joshua 1:9

I wrote earlier that although every human being on this planet has an inherent call to leadership, most of us do not have the courage or the conviction to capture it. This is a serious problem. We've been so conditioned by discouragement, failure, or the oppression of others that we are afraid to follow our natural leadership instincts given to us at creation. We make excuses, such as "I'm too shy," "I'm not as gifted as he is," "I don't have the education," "My family was never good at that," and so on.

All of us must capture and cultivate the leadership spirit—this attitude of shaping and forming our lives according to our God-given purposes. Sadly, relatively few people in the entire human race ever capture or discover the spirit of leadership to the point where they ignite their leadership potential. Our greatest challenge is to nurture our inherent leadership instincts to the extent that we can rise from being followers to being leaders in our personal domains. This takes conviction, powered by purpose.

The leadership potential within you is waiting to be discovered. Remember, true leadership is *self-discovery*. It has very little to do with what you *do* but is fundamentally a matter of becoming who you *are*. It is the result of one's commitment to self-manifestation.

When you make the decision to cultivate your intrinsic leadership potential, a transition will occur. You will gain conviction, becoming like the young lion who left the sheep pen and went into the forest so that he could fulfill his true nature. Did he face the uncertainty, challenges, and dangers of the forest? Yes. But he also became what he was designed to be. He learned, grew, and became a leader by discovering the potential within himself.

The lion who lived on the farm was always a lion, but because he grew up in an environment that was unnatural to him, he thought he was a sheep. Our environment (our education, social training, cultures, nations, or families) has been defining us and giving us the parameters of what we can and can't be. The only way to counter this often unnatural information is to discover our true selves by seeing a picture of our leadership nature so that we can know who we really are. Once the young lion saw the older lion, he knew what he was supposed to become, and he gained the conviction to act on it.

Sometimes we think, "If someone tells me that I'm a leader, then, okay, I'm a leader." No, you *are* a leader. The first issue is whether or not you will discover this truth for yourself. The second issue is whether you will manifest who you really are with conviction. The purpose of this devotional is to give you two things: the information to discover your leadership nature and the revelation of what it means to develop and live out your leadership potential. My deepest desire is to give you a picture of your true self so that you can start on the journey to fulfilling it.

Have you made a commitment to self-manifestation?

Thought: You were *born* to lead, but you must *become* a leader.

Reading: Joshua 1:1–9

—DAY 24—

THE POWER OF VISION

"Where there is no vision, the people perish."
—Proverbs 29:18 (KJV)

How do you progress from discovering your purpose and developing conviction to having a vision? Let's look briefly at the distinction between purpose and vision. Having a *sense of purpose* means knowing and understanding what you were born to accomplish. Having a *vision* means seeing the outworking and details of that purpose in your mind by faith and beginning to imagine it as reality.

As you seek to learn (or recover) your purpose, again ask yourself questions such as these: "What have I always wanted to do? What thoughts, ideas, plans, and dreams have remained consistent within me?" Once you answer these questions, you can begin to formulate your vision by considering, "What specifically can I do to fulfill my plans and dreams?" When you start to see your vision clearly, you will be able to follow your life's purpose as a leader. This vision must be very plain to you because you need something specific to work toward; otherwise, you will risk not accomplishing your purpose.

I am commonly asked this question: "How can I know if my vision as a leader is inspired by God and merits the support of many people?" The question is really one of motivation. My answer is a result of having questioned myself many years ago when I wanted to determine whether my personal passion, desires, and vision in life were divinely inspired. After much contemplation and prayer, I received an answer that has guided me for nearly forty years. The answer was simple: Does your vision improve, enhance, and help humanity? Does your passion make human life better on planet earth and relieve mankind of things that tear down and destroy?

This answer provides the criteria for all personal dreams, passions, desires, and plans. If your purpose, vision, and goals benefit only you, then they are not divinely inspired. True leadership will always result in the advancement, development, enhancement, improvement, protection, and security of humanity. Leadership inspired by God never destroys but is constructive and progressive. Any desire to lead that does not include empowering others and improving their lives is selfish ambition, and this type of ambition has no place in leadership.

Vision also requires commitment. Some people have visions concerning their purpose without the will to bring them into reality. An effective leader not only develops a specific vision, but they also make a strong commitment to it born of conviction. Jesus expressed this perspective when He said, in effect, "My food is to do the will of My father." (See John 4:34.) Committing to your vision will enable you to stay the course with your purpose rather than be distracted by lesser (even if good) or unnecessary things.

A leader recognizes that the tone and standards they set for the accomplishment of their vision have a direct bearing on their ability to empower others. If they influence in a positive way other people who share their vision, progress will be made. If they resort to authoritarian power, unjust practices, or carelessness, they jeopardize the vision. The quality and integrity of daily advancement toward the vision are their responsibility.

⌒

Thought: An effective leader not only develops a specific vision but also makes a strong commitment to it.

Readings: Psalm 20:4; Proverbs 16:3

THE POWER OF PASSION

"Never be lacking in zeal [passion], but keep your spiritual fervor, serving the Lord."   —Romans 12:11

Passion is the generator of the energy and resilience of a leader. A passionate commitment to a purpose allows a true leader to defy opposition, adversity, failure, disappointment, and discouragement.

Passion is a controlling desire that exceeds the boundaries of casual interest or concern and transports you into the realm of obligation. In other words, leadership is discovering a sense of significance to one's generation and making a commitment to deliver that significance as an obligation. In essence, true leadership passion is the discovery of a belief, reason, idea, conviction, or cause not just to live for but also to die for, which focuses on benefiting mankind. It is this sense of personal resolve, obligation, and willingness to sacrifice personal advantage, comfort, and advancement for the sake of a noble cause that impacts others and resonates within them a desire to help achieve the stated desire, goal, or vision.

True leaders, therefore, are those who effectively express their inner passions, which then find a common response in the hearts of others. It is passion that attracts people to the leader, who motivates them to take action. This vital aspect of effective leadership development was expressed in the lives of all great leaders throughout history and identifies what separates them from their followers.

This is why true leaders are willing to die for their life's purpose. Dr. Martin Luther King Jr. once said, "I submit to you that if a man hasn't discovered something he will die for, he isn't fit to live."[7]

The greatest example of one who had a passionate purpose stronger than death is Jesus Christ. He said to His disciples, *"Greater love has no one than this: to lay down one's life for one's friends"* (John 15:13). The power of Jesus's life, death, and resurrection changed the course of history, reconciled untold numbers of people to their Creator, and gave humanity eternal hope for the future.

Jesus's leadership effectiveness is undisputed even by His critics and skeptics, and no study of historical leaders can be fairly conducted without reference to His impeccable achievement and His model as a leader of the highest order. No man has ever affected the destiny and development of humanity as this one has.

Jesus was so passionate about what He came to do that He motivated His disciples to leave behind their old priorities and ways of living in order to discover a new kind of life with Him. They had never met anyone who was ready to die for what He was living for. Moreover, Jesus's impact and imprint on the history of the world and on the personal lives of hundreds of millions over two millennia testify of leadership in its essence and at its highest level.

⌣

Thought: When a person discovers a sense of purpose, it produces a passion for pursuing it, and that passion is what inspires other people to want to join in the pursuit.

Reading: Psalm 63:1–5

---

7. Martin Luther King Jr., speech in Detroit, Michigan, June 23, 1963, in *Oxford Essential Quotations*, 5th ed., ed. Susan Ratcliffe (Oxford: Oxford University Press, 2017), Oxford Reference, https://www.oxfordreference.com/display/10.1093/acref/9780191843730.001.0001/q-oro-ed5-00006293.

— Day 26 —
WHAT IS PASSION?

"For when I preach the gospel, I cannot boast, since I am compelled to preach. Woe to me if I do not preach the gospel!"
—1 Corinthians 9:16

Today, let's further explore what it means to have leadership passion. Passion may be defined in the following ways:

A deep desire. Passion is stamina that says, "I'm going to go after this, no matter what happens. If I have to wait ten years, I'm going to get it." If you want to go all the way to your dream, you can't sit back and expect everything to be easy. True leaders possess a deep desire that produces the passion to proceed with their dreams.

A "craving." Passionate people are "possessed" people. In other words, you can't be successful as a leader unless you have a real inner need to accomplish something very specific.

An obligation. When you are passionate about something, you feel compelled to do it. Again, leadership is born when someone discovers a divine obligation to their community, world, and generation. As the apostle Paul wrote, *"For when I preach the gospel, I cannot boast, since I am compelled to preach. Woe to me if I do not preach the gospel!"* (1 Corinthians 9:16).

A deep commitment. Many people are "interested" in doing certain things, but they aren't really committed to accomplishing them. Some people say that they will get a better job, lose weight, or change their lives in other ways—someday. The world is filled with people who are merely interested but not passionate. Commitment is the guy who jumps out of an airplane, trusting that the parachute will open. It's not talk but action. Passion makes you jump in, no matter what.

Leaders are willing to put their whole selves into accomplishing their purposes. Remember, true leadership is not finding something to live for but something to die for.

A deep resolution. We make New Year's resolutions every year and quickly forget them. How determined are you? Do you act on what you've committed yourself to do? Are you willing to pay the price to obtain your desire? True leaders are resolved in their decisions to pursue their purposes and goals.

A deep motivation. Passion is the juice for living. For many people, life is a drudgery. They have no motivation in regard to their jobs, spouses, education, or personal development. Someone once said that the thing about life is that it is so daily. Passion helps us to rise above our daily routines.

If you're not motivated, then you will become a weight or burden to others. You will pull on their energy. Passion is a source of motivation. When you have passion, you don't need the right conditions to move forward because passion is internally generated; it is not affected by external conditions. True leaders do not need outside stimuli in order to take action. They are self-motivated.

⌐

Thought: Leaders are willing to put their whole selves into accomplishing their purposes.

Reading: 1 Corinthians 9:16–18

THE POWER OF INSPIRATION

*"Therefore encourage one another and build each other up,
just as in fact you are doing."*   —1 Thessalonians 5:11

Over the last several days of devotions, we have been following
the progression of leadership development. So far, we have focused
on *purpose, conviction,* and *passion.* All these elements are essential,
but I believe the greatest and most important aspect of leadership
is *inspiration.* The principal pursuit, therefore, for those who desire
and aspire to become effective leaders must be the answer to this
question: "How do I inspire?"

The source of true inspiration is our Creator, and He is therefore the source of genuine leadership. Inspiration is the opposite
of intimidation and is absent of manipulation. There are many
so-called leadership situations in which the motivation for the followers is a fear of the one in charge rather than a commitment
based on a response to an inspired life. Inspiration is the capacity
to cause others to discover themselves, their purposes, and their
abilities, and to maximize their potential.

In essence, inspirational power is the ability to successfully
communicate one's passion to others. True inspiration is not using
people or brainwashing them. Instead, it is an invitation to pursue
something higher and better than one has had before and, in the
process, gain a sense of meaning and significance for one's life. This
component of inspiration is at the heart of influence in leadership.

Leadership can be summarized as contagious inspiration.
After a vision is ignited in the heart of the leader and catches on
in the hearts of others, it begins to be carried along by the energy

and momentum of people who envision the possibilities of a better future, a more effective product, a new cure, a more enriching environment, a life-changing perspective, or a renewed life. In my experience, inspiration is the most important force in leadership not only because it motivates, but also because it protects the leader from the temptation to manipulate others.

Let's go back once more to the definition of true leadership: *Leadership is the capacity **to influence others through inspiration** motivated by a passion, generated by a vision, produced by a conviction, ignited by a purpose.* If inspiration is the key to legitimate influence and thus the source of true leadership, then, as I expressed at the beginning of this devotion, genuine inspiration must be the pursuit of all true leaders.

⌇

Thought: Inspirational power is the ability to successfully communicate one's passion to others.

Reading: 1 Thessalonians 5:11–15

— Day 28 —

THIS IS INSPIRATION!

"Let us consider how we may spur one another on toward love and good deeds."   —Hebrews 10:24

The key to mobilizing others is inspiration. *If you can inspire, you can mobilize.* This is leadership.

David of Bethlehem, despite his youth and lack of military experience, and without formal training or mentoring, believed that he could beat the odds and defeat a nine-foot giant, thereby saving the dignity and integrity of his nation. He later became the greatest king of Israel. *This is inspiration.*

Outside the biblical text, there are historical examples of others who have been inspired by their visions of a preferred future. Florence Nightingale was born into a family of wealth and privilege, but she believed she had a calling from God. She devoted her life to improving standards of medical care for both soldiers and civilians, as well as to providing exceptional nurses' training for women. *This is inspiration.*

Mahatma Gandhi was only five foot five and weighed roughly a hundred pounds, yet he seemed to bear the weight of millions of his people in India who were crushed under the burden of a colonial empire. He believed that he could face the giant of Great Britain and deliver his people to a better future. *This is inspiration.*

Nelson Mandela was a simple African lawyer who returned from a respected university in England to his apartheid-oppressed people. He was lifted to a place where he saw a South Africa in which all men were equal, dignified, and free. He was willing to sacrifice the most valuable years of his life in a prison cell for the sake of this dream. *This is inspiration.*

Mother Teresa left her teaching job because she envisioned a ministry of serving the "poorest of the poor" in India. In the process, she brought worldwide attention to the plight of the outcast, sick, and destitute. She sparked the same vision in the hearts of many other people who continue to bring care and dignity to those whom society has discarded. *This is inspiration.*

Inspiration is at the heart of true leadership, and the breath of the Spirit of God is the source of inspiration. This is why, to be the leader that the Creator intended you to be, you must have a personal relationship with God through His Son Jesus Christ. Allow Him to breathe into your being a purpose and vision for your life that will strengthen your faith and activate a passion in your heart to accomplish your dream. This soul-inspiring vision and passionate drive to fulfill a call will transform you from a follower into a leader. A true leader's work is not a job or career but the very life you live in becoming what God made you to be.

⌒

Thought: The key to mobilizing others is inspiration. *If you can inspire, you can mobilize.*

Reading: Hebrews 10:19–25

— Day 29 —

THE POWER OF INFLUENCE

"Let your light so shine before men, that they may see your good works and glorify your Father in heaven."
— Matthew 5:16 (NKJV)

The purest form of leadership is influence through inspiration. It may take the form of the influence of one friend on another, one spouse on another, a parent on a child, a teacher on students, a pastor on a congregation, a supervisor on employees, a community leader on volunteers, or a governmental leader on an entire nation of people.

As I expressed earlier, an individual's vision, when fully possessed and matured, explodes in a passion that creates an internal drive in the individual and inspires all who come into their presence. It is this capacity of the individual's passion to inspire that produces *influence*, the foundational component of leadership.

Leadership is therefore measured by the degree to which one can influence others. It is what people give to you after you have influenced them by your passion to the point where you have inspired them.

Leadership is the ability to influence the priorities of many people toward a shared cause that is nobler than the private pursuits of the individuals involved. In his book *Spiritual Leadership*, J. Oswald Sanders quoted British field marshal Bernard Montgomery, who said, "Leadership is the capacity and will to rally men and women to a common purpose, and the character which inspires confidence."[8] Leadership is also coordinating the diverse gifts and talents of individuals for a corporate goal, as well as organizing resources, energies, and relationships in a productive context to achieve an intended result.

Leadership's true influence must derive its power from strong values, deep convictions, and firm principles. Having a God-inspired vision and values leads to inspiring and motivating others to work together with a common purpose. Leadership influences people to maximize their own potential and that of the resources they administer. Thus, purpose and vision are the sources from which leadership derives its magnetic field to activate the commitment, cooperation, and confidence of others.

Thought: Leadership is what people give to you after you have influenced them by your passion to the point where you have inspired them.

Reading: Matthew 5:13–14

---

8. Bernard L. Montgomery, *Memoirs of Field-Marshal Montgomery* (Cleveland: World, 1958), 70, in J. Oswald Sanders, *Spiritual Leadership: A Commitment to Excellence for Every Believer* (Chicago: Moody Publishers, 2007), 27.

— DAY 30 —
INFLUENCE, NOT MANIPULATION

"Like a roaring lion or a charging bear is a wicked ruler over a helpless people."   —Proverbs 28:15

A vital leadership question remains: What is the *source* of your influence on others?

There seems to be a deep desire in the unregenerate spirit of humanity—that which has not been reconciled to the Creator and is not being guided by His Spirit—to dominate others and to use power for other selfish purposes. History is full of case studies of people who rose to powerful leadership positions through both legitimate and illegitimate means and then began to expose the dark motives of their hearts. Their immoral motives resulted in the suffering, abuse, and destruction of millions of innocent lives.

These people, both past and present, have influenced others using threats and violence, but we don't call that true leadership; we call it manipulation, oppression, or dictatorship. For example, Nero, Hitler, Stalin, Mao Zedong, and Idi Amin were all influential by exerting their wills over people; however, they were not leaders in the true sense.

Adolf Hitler came to office promising the German people a return to their former glory as a nation. Yet, once he was führer, his distorted values and desire for self-glorification grew increasingly clear as he persecuted European citizens for his own selfish purposes, instigated the Second World War, and ordered the annihilation of millions of Jews and others. The leaders of the Russian Revolution promised equality for all citizens, but the aftermath under the Soviet Union was decades of oppression of the country's people and a waste of generations of potential.

This type of "leadership" is only a flaunting of dangerous, authoritarian power, characterized by the following:

A controlling atmosphere. Some people "lead" by promoting an environment of fear, intimidation, obligation, dependency, or guilt.

A discouragement of creativity and individuality. Ideas are imposed from the top down, and there is no room for the contribution of ideas and solutions by subordinates.

A lack of teamwork. When people are not encouraged to work together, are pitted against one another, and are excluded from the mission of a company or organization, they will usually retreat into their "corners" and take on an attitude of self-preservation. This separation and estrangement can lead to suspicion, apathy, power struggles, and decreased productivity.

An absence of appreciation and credit. Authoritarian power is not concerned with the contributions of subordinates except to make sure that they have completed their tasks. Those who wield such power don't credit those who have played a role in successes, but they are quick to blame others when there are mistakes.

Authoritarian power and influence nullify people's potential and stifle them spiritually, emotionally, mentally, and sometimes physically. In every area of life, there are people who aspire to positions of leadership and influence motivated by selfish ambitions. They may not go to the extreme of persecuting or murdering people, but their selfish ambition causes other types of human and social destruction.

In God's leadership plan, you do not need to manipulate, intimidate, or coerce anyone. True leadership elicits other people's willing submission of their authority to yours, motivated by Holy Spirit-led influence.

⌒

Thought: What is the source of your influence on others?

Reading: Proverbs 28:14–16

— Day 31 —

THE LEADERSHIP SPIRIT AND LOVE

"Dear friends, since God so loved us, we also ought to love one another."   —1 John 4:11

I trust that by now you understand your leadership spirit is inherent and that self-discovery is at the heart of activating this leadership spirit. This self-discovery is birthed from recognizing your true nature, potential, capacity, character, and abilities through rediscovering your Source—God. This will naturally lead you to the revelation that *all humans* are created in God's image and likeness, and therefore possess the same value, worth, and estimation as yourself.

Thus, if each individual bears the same image of God that you do, it becomes impossible to separate His image in man from Himself. In essence, it is not possible to say that you *love* God but *hate* mankind, for this becomes a contradiction. The apostle John made this very clear: *"Whoever does not love their brother and sister, whom they have seen, cannot love God, whom they have not seen"* (1 John 4:20).

If you believe in God's purpose for all of mankind in creation, you will have a natural love for others because you will perceive that you and they are essentially the same. Since they are made in God's image and likeness, as you are, then any negative approach or act against them is an act against yourself and against the Creator, as well.

True leaders who are connected with their inherent leadership spirit understand that serving mankind is serving God Himself, and thus serve their fellow men from a motivation of love and respect. We see this principle in the following expressions in the Bible:

Whoever does not love does not know God, because God is love. (1 John 4:8)

We love because he first loved us. Whoever claims to love God yet hates a brother or sister is a liar. For whoever does not love their brother and sister, whom they have seen, cannot love God, whom they have not seen. And he has given us this command: Anyone who loves God must also love their brother and sister. (1 John 4:19–21)

Jesus replied: "'Love the Lord your God with all your heart and with all your soul and with all your mind.' This is the first and greatest commandment. And the second is like it: 'Love your neighbor as yourself.' All the Law and the Prophets hang on these two commandments." (Matthew 22:37–40)

These verses clearly indicate that love for mankind is a priority and is evidence that you love God, the Creator of humanity. Certainly, this is a major ingredient missing in leadership today. The current focus is on results, performance, and competition much more than on values, such as love, caring, compassion, serving, and kindness. We need leaders who love others more than they love their goals and objectives. Each of us must understand and capture this leadership spirit so that we may honor God, love others, and fully manifest the leadership potential hidden within us.

Thought: All humans are created in God's image and likeness, and therefore possess the same value, worth, and estimation as yourself.

Reading: 1 John 4:7–21

—DAY 32—

THE SECRET TO GREATNESS

"The Son of Man did not come to be served, but to serve, and to give his life as a ransom for many."   —Matthew 20:28

Since we are leaders by nature, the desire to lead and achieve greatness is natural, even though many of us deny that this silent, passionate longing exists in every human heart. Leadership is your desire and your destiny. Leadership by God's design also has a *secret ingredient.*

Our model leader, Jesus Christ, had an interesting encounter with His disciples, a small group of men whom He had chosen to train as leaders. His "training school" lasted three years, and, as we have already noted, His success as a mentor and trainer is evidenced by the successful impact His students have had on the world and on human development over the past two thousand years. Let's listen in on one of their conversations, which Jesus used as an opportunity to teach about the definition and precepts of true leadership.

In the New Testament, there is an account of a request that was made to Jesus by two of His disciples who were in His leadership training school. It is recorded like this:

> *Then the mother of Zebedee's sons came to Jesus with her sons and, kneeling down, asked a favor of him. "What is it you want?" he asked. She said, "Grant that one of these two sons of mine may sit at your right and the other at your left in your kingdom." "You don't know what you are asking," Jesus said to them. "Can you drink the cup I am going to drink?" "We can," they answered. Jesus said to them, "You will indeed*

drink from my cup, but to sit at my right or left is not for me to grant. These places belong to those for whom they have been prepared by my Father." When the ten heard about this, they were indignant with the two brothers. Jesus called them together and said, "You know that the rulers of the Gentiles lord it over them, and their high officials exercise authority over them. Not so with you." (Matthew 20:20–26)

Next, Jesus made an amazing statement. Please note that He did not rebuke the brothers for desiring to be great and seeking leadership positions. As a matter of fact, with the following statement, He went even further and showed them *how* to become great. Why didn't He rebuke them? Because Jesus knew and understood the nature and inherent passion of human beings to lead.

Instead, whoever wants to become great among you must be your servant, and whoever wants to be first must be your slave—just as the Son of Man did not come to be served, but to serve, and to give his life as a ransom for many.
(Matthew 20:26–28)

I believe that this story contains the greatest secret of true leadership, as well as the process necessary for becoming a genuine leader. With His answer to this question of greatness, Jesus expressed the key, the nature, and the process for you to discover and manifest your true leadership spirit: the secret is serving others.

Thought: Jesus understood the nature and inherent passion of human beings to lead.

Reading: Philippians 2:3–4

— DAY 33 —

WHAT DO I SERVE TO OTHERS?

"Each of you should use whatever gift you have received to serve others, as faithful stewards of God's grace in its various forms." —1 Peter 4:10

W hat do I serve to others?" I believe this is the greatest revelation of true leadership I have ever discovered and exceeds all the theories and research from the past. In effect, what Jesus was stating in Matthew 20:26, *"Whoever wants to become great among you must be your servant"*—which is also reflected in the above verse from 1 Peter 4:10—is that to become the great leader you were destined to be, you must discover your unique gift and assignment (your original purpose) and *serve that to the world.* Do not seek greatness, but instead seek to serve your gift to others to the maximum extent that you can, and you will both glorify God and become a sought-after person.

Jesus defined true leadership as becoming a person who is valuable to others, rather than a person of just position or fame. If you find your unique gift or special talent and commit to serving it to the world, then your significance will cause people to seek you out. The more you become a person whose gift is valued, the greater your influence will be.

Therefore, the hidden strength of true leadership is knowing your gifts and then serving yourself to the world. When you do this effectively, people will call you a leader. Genuine leadership is not measured by how many people serve you but by how many people you serve. The greater your service, the greater your value to others, and the greater your leadership. My admonition to you is not to seek greatness but to serve your way to leadership.

Remember, Jesus used Himself as an example of serving by saying, *"The Son of Man did not come to be served, but to serve, and to give his life as a ransom for many"* (Matthew 20:28). In other words, He was explaining what makes a person great in the kingdom of God. Essentially, Jesus was saying, "Study Me. What is My gift? What did I come into the world to do? What is My purpose? What is My assignment?" Jesus came to be a ransom or substitute for the many so that we might benefit from His sacrifice. Therefore, He was saying to us, "See? That's how you become a true leader. I'm fulfilling My purpose. I'm serving Myself to the world and giving My life for the benefit of others. I'm serving as a ransom for everybody so that they can be set free."

Jesus is also essentially saying to us, "Find what you're supposed to do, and serve it to others. Then you'll become great."

Let's return to the question "What do I serve to others?" Whatever we were created to do, God built us for. Again, we can often tell what our leadership domain is by what talents and abilities we are naturally designed with. They indicate the area(s) that we are supposed to have dominion in—our domain. Find your domain and serve it to the world. Others have been waiting for your gift all your life. Therefore, lead through service.

⌒

Thought: The shortest distance to leadership is service.

Reading: 1 Peter 4:10–11

— DAY 34 —

YOUR SELF-WORTH IN GOD

"What, then, shall we say in response to these things? If God is for us, who can be against us?" —Romans 8:31

Knowing that you have been created by God for a specific purpose sets you free from the negative effects of other people's opinions. That is the reason why you can serve people as a servant leader. Even if they mistreat you, it doesn't affect your estimation of your value to them. This is why Jesus Christ could say on the cross, *"Father, forgive them, for they do not know what they are doing"* (Luke 23:34). He knew how valuable He was to them—both in who He was and in what He was doing on their behalf. His understanding of His purpose and His worth to the Father was intact right to the end.

True leaders capture their leadership spirit out of a strong sense of self-worth and self-esteem based on their understanding that we were created in the image of God. As a result, true leaders can be compassionate, patient, forgiving, and kind. They do not need to gain their self-assessment from the people whom they are serving. They understand that you cannot set people free until you are free from them. If you need the people whom you are leading in order to feel important, then you cannot truly lead them. Ultimately, they will end up leading you.

A true leader seeks approval from God rather than adulation from people. Leaders who know who they are do not depend on others to validate their sense of self-worth. Yet they also have to be careful not to encourage and embrace an overestimation of themselves by their followers, especially to the point where they, rather than the vision, become the focus of attention. When a leader encourages such adulation, it is often a manifestation of insecurity. True leaders understand that any measure of popularity they have is simply a temporary reaction of people to their gifts and positions and does not reflect who they are as people. They are more concerned about pleasing God than about being popular with others. They have "an audience of One," as some have called it. They do not confuse applause with affirmation. They do not confuse temporary awards with eternal reward.

This is why discovering the leadership spirit is a prerequisite to serving. If you never discover who you are, you will always misinterpret the attitudes and actions of others. You'll also underestimate everyone else—you'll consider them less than what they really are because you'll want to feel that you are above them. You will "under-esteem" them. However, you will treat people well and esteem them highly when you discover the leadership spirit and are secure in God's purpose and plan for you.

⌒

Thought: A true leader is more concerned about pleasing God than about being popular with people.

Reading: Galatians 1:10

—Day 35—

IGNITING THE SPIRIT OF LEADERSHIP

"When they saw the courage of Peter and John and realized that they were unschooled, ordinary men, they were astonished and they took note that these men had been with Jesus."
—Acts 4:13

By now you understand that the *leadership spirit* refers to the inherent spirit in mankind that possesses the natural qualities and characteristics of the Creator. Our having the leadership spirit means that we are naturally created to lead. Discovering the truth about the leadership spirit means we know *who we are*. Yet, as we have learned, while every human being possesses this spirit, very few ever discover this truth, and fewer still are aware they can manifest their leadership spirit.

I have distinguished between the *leadership spirit* and the *spirit of leadership* so that you can better understand your leadership potential. The spirit of leadership is the consciousness of having been made in the image of the Creator, as well as the attitudes that accompany that awareness. The spirit of leadership is a derivative of the leadership spirit. However, the concepts are different in that the spirit of leadership refers to the *mindset* and *attitudes* we must acquire in order for the leadership spirit to be activated and manifested. Without the spirit of leadership, your leadership spirit will remain dormant. We see in the description of Peter and John in Acts 4:13 that they had truly discovered the spirit of leadership: *"When they saw the courage of Peter and John and realized that they were unschooled, ordinary men, they were astonished and they took note that these men had been with Jesus."*

Thus, even though you are inherently a leader through God's design, there are some additional qualities that you need to discover and develop in order to operate as a leader. To manifest the spirit of leadership, you must *choose* to fulfill your leadership nature. Having the leadership spirit without the spirit of leadership is like having a powerful automobile without the knowledge or ability to drive it. Or it is like a seed that never becomes the tree it was destined to be.

To use another analogy, at some point, a mother bird will nudge her baby birds out of the nest, as if to say, "You need to do what you were naturally born to do," and the baby birds will either start flying or risk falling out of the nest. The same is true for you in the sense that you are naturally a leader, and you can "fly" once you tap into what you were born to do. Manifesting the spirit of leadership is a matter of discovering and nurturing your true self so that you evidence your leadership nature.

Twelve powerful attitudes or qualities of the spirit of leadership are purpose, passion, initiative, priorities, goal-setting, teamwork, innovation, accountability, persistence, self-discipline, self-cultivation, and mentorship of your successors. This section of the devotional is dedicated to helping you capture the essence of the *mental framework* and *accompanying attitudes* that will ignite the spirit of leadership within you.

⸻

Thought: The spirit of leadership is not a method, a technique, or a science but the power of your mindset and your attitude.

Reading: Acts 4:1–13

— Day 36 —

YOU ARE WHAT YOU THINK

"For as he thinks in his heart, so is he."
—Proverbs 23:7 (NKJV)

The spirit of leadership is the state of mind or attitude that emanates from the nature of a leader. There is nothing on earth as powerful as a thought or an idea. We are what we think, and we become what we continue to think.

No one can rise above the plane of their mental conditioning. We must cultivate a personal environment that is conducive to producing the mentality and attitudes necessary for our leadership potential to be ignited. This is the spirit of leadership. As we have seen, true leadership has more to do with mindset than with methods and techniques. To change your life, *you must change your mind.*

This is why Paul wrote to the Romans, *"Do not conform to the pattern of this world, but be transformed by the renewing of your mind"* (Romans 12:2). It is also why the apostle Peter wrote, *"So prepare your minds for action and exercise self-control"* (1 Peter 1:13 NLT).

We can look at the spirit of leadership from various definitions and perspectives that will help us to grasp this vital concept. The *spirit of leadership:*

- Is your mindset
- Is your mental conditioning
- Is your thoughts about yourself and your environment.
- Is revealed in your response to your environment
- Is a perception of yourself and the world

- Includes the convictions that regulate your thoughts about yourself and your world
- Is your personal, private philosophy of life
- Is your belief system, which controls your behavior
- Dictates your motivation
- Is the source of your actions, which determines the response of the environment (in other words, your attitude often determines how other people treat you and how the world responds to you)
- Is how you interpret the world

This idea bears repeating: *You are what you believe.* Your thoughts create your beliefs, your beliefs create your convictions, your convictions create your attitude, your attitude controls your perception, and your perception dictates your behavior. What you truly believe about yourself creates your world. Remember that no one can live beyond the limits of their beliefs. Thus, your life is what you *think* it should be.

Thought: We are what we think, and we become what we continue to think.

Reading: Philippians 4:8–9

— DAY 37 —

THE SOURCE OF YOUR THOUGHTS

"Those who live according to the flesh have their minds set on what the flesh desires; but those who live in accordance with the Spirit have their minds set on what the Spirit desires."
—Romans 8:5

While it is true that there is nothing as powerful as a thought or idea, there is nothing more important than the *source* of our thoughts. Our thoughts are products of what we have heard or learned. What we derive our thoughts from determines the kind of thoughts we conceive and who we eventually become. If it is true that *"as* [a person] *thinks in his heart, so is he"* (Proverbs 23:7 NKJV), then the source from which we get our thoughts is most critical.

Therefore, as we approach this subject of the spirit of leadership—essentially, the thought-life of the individual—we must carefully consider the process by which thoughts transfer to our lives. That process involves the following:

1. A source transmits its ideas through words or images.

2. Words heard or images seen transmit thoughts and ideas to our minds.

3. Thoughts conceived become ideas.

4. Ideas conceived become ideologies.

5. Ideologies conceived become beliefs.

6. Beliefs conceived become convictions.

7. Convictions conceived become philosophies.

8. Philosophies conceived become lifestyles.

9. Lifestyles determine our destinies.

A careful study of the above process reveals that the most important component is *the source of our thoughts*. As a result, our mindsets, attitudes, beliefs, and convictions are generally determined by someone else's ideas. It is remarkable that you and I can be living what other people think about life or about us. Therefore, the key to living effectively is to receive your thoughts from the correct source.

When your philosophy, beliefs, thoughts, and convictions are based on the way God created you to think, and on the thoughts He communicates to you through His Word, you will naturally rule over your environment and fulfill your life's purpose. When they are based on erroneous thinking and attitudes, you will feel frustrated and trapped by your circumstances. Unfortunately, this is the case for too many people. That is why I often say that *there is a leader trapped in every follower.*

Your mind matters, and it controls how you manage your life. If you truly understand what it means to be made in the likeness of God, then you will come to possess the powerful mindset and attitudes that encompass the spirit of leadership.

Thought: There is nothing more important than the source of our thoughts.

Reading: Romans 8:5–9

— DAY 38 —
WHAT IS YOUR VALUE?

*"How precious to me are your thoughts, God! How vast is the
sum of them!"*   —Psalm 139:17

When we consider the source of our thoughts, we need to
revisit the relationship between God and our self-concept. Your
mindset and attitudes are largely a result of your self-concept—the
picture you have of yourself. What idea do you have about who
and what you are? The answer to this question is crucial because
your self-perception influences whether you will walk in the power
of the spirit of leadership.

Your self-worth is the value you place on yourself. How much
value do you think you have? Since the Creator made you in His
image and likeness, your value is a reflection of *His value*. He wants
you to have a concept of yourself that is in line with who He is.
That is the picture you are meant to have of yourself. Families pass
down certain genes and traits from one generation to the next.
Similarly, our Father God passed along His nature to us, and that
"family resemblance" is meant to be a reminder of where we come
from, to whom we belong, and what we are intended to be. *"Yet
you, Lord, are our Father. We are the clay, you are the potter; we are
all the work of your hand"* (Isaiah 64:8).

Unfortunately, the majority of the people in the world do not
have self-worth but "others-worth." This is the acceptance of the
worth others place on you. You will never become the leader you
were created to be until you become free from other people's valuation of you and perception of your worth. Leaders value others as
they value themselves.

If a person has power but does not possess a sound self-concept or self-image, then they will relate to others from that distorted perspective. This insecurity will manifest itself in fear, suspicion, distrust, and hatred of self and others. A poor self-concept will result in a low valuation of humanity, and it becomes the source of abuse, corruption, oppression, and the need to dominate and control others.

The essence of the spirit of leadership is that you give *other* people value. In other words, you give them something valuable to contribute to and become involved in. True leadership gives people a cause, a reason for living, and a sense of significance that gives meaning to their lives so that they feel necessary and purposeful. It gives them an outlet for expressing their own gifting. You cannot give significance to others if you don't already understand your significance in God. You cannot lead people where you have not gone yourself.

Thought: The foundation of the spirit of leadership is a sound self-concept based on who God has created you to be.

Reading: Psalm 139:13–18

— DAY 39 —

"LOVE YOUR NEIGHBOR AS YOURSELF"

"And the second [greatest commandment] is like it: 'Love your neighbor as yourself.'"　　　　　—Matthew 22:39

In the book of Deuteronomy, we find these words: *"Love the LORD your God with all your heart and with all your soul and with all your strength"* (Deuteronomy 6:5). In the New Testament, Jesus repeated this Scripture when He was asked, in effect, "What is the most important duty of all mankind?" Jesus replied that the first and greatest commandment is to love God with all your being, and that the second great commandment is like it: *"Love your neighbor as yourself"* (Matthew 22:39; Mark 12:31; Luke 10:27).

Most of us have missed the fact that "love your neighbor" is a leadership statement. If you consider Jesus's words carefully, He wasn't telling us to love our neighbors first. Essentially, He was saying that we must love ourselves first. We can love our neighbors only to the degree that we love ourselves.

Therefore, a healthy intrapersonal relationship is a prerequisite for effective interpersonal relationships. Your attitude toward others is a reflection of your attitude toward yourself. This means that if we don't get our attitudes toward ourselves right, then we're going to have the wrong attitudes when interacting with others. It is imperative that leaders possess a healthy, wholesome love for themselves first in order to lead others effectively. We must remember this: *often, whatever you believe about yourself, you will believe about other people.*

The command from Deuteronomy to *"love the LORD your God with all your heart and with all your soul and with all your strength"* has to do with discovering the nature of the Creator. If you are pursuing God, His Word, and what Jesus Christ has done for you with everything you have, then you will discover both God and yourself. When this happens, as I wrote earlier, you will realize that everyone else on earth is made in God's image, just as you are, and therefore they possess the same value, worth, and estimation. When I love others, I am loving myself and God because we all have the same nature.

Again, our self-esteem should be equal to the esteem with which the Creator regards us. He esteemed us so much that He sent His Son to die for us so that we could have eternal life with Him. (See John 3:16.) God esteemed us so much that He gave us the authority and the ability to govern over creation, making us coleaders and corulers with Him on earth. (See Genesis 1:26.)

When you come to know your Creator, and finally come to know yourself, and when you live according to that knowledge, then your spirit of leadership is ignited. Your attitudes are adjusted. Your beliefs about yourself, mankind, and your role in the world are radically transformed. You become the leader God foresaw since the beginning of time.

Thought: Our self-esteem should be equal to the esteem with which the Creator regards us.

Reading: Matthew 22:34–40

— Day 40 —

ATTITUDE AND BEHAVIOR ARE RELATED

"I the Lord search the heart and examine the mind, to reward each person according to their conduct, according to what their deeds deserve." —Jeremiah 17:10

The prophet Jeremiah recorded these words of God: *"I the Lord search the heart and examine the mind, to reward each person according to their conduct, according to what their deeds deserve"* (Jeremiah 17:10). The Creator examines the seat of people's attitudes and sees what is stored there. He does this to reward them according to what? Their conduct or behavior. Attitude and behavior are tied together because our actions come from what we think.

The writer of Hebrews said, *"The word of God is alive and active. Sharper than any double-edged sword, it penetrates even to dividing soul and spirit, joints and marrow; it judges the thoughts and attitudes of the heart"* (Hebrews 4:12). We are held accountable not only for our actions but also for our thoughts and attitudes. In the Old Testament, God reminded the prophet Samuel, *"People look at the outward appearance, but the Lord looks at the heart"* (1 Samuel 16:7). This is because the subconscious mind reveals what a person really is within.

Matthew's gospel records Jesus's words as He addressed the principle of focus: *"Where your treasure is, there your heart will be also"* (Matthew 6:21). Here is the principle: *Whatever you value will preoccupy your mind, thoughts, and conscience.* For instance, if you value earthly wealth more than the higher ideals of spiritual purity, goodness, kindness, faithfulness, and other noble attributes, then this will be your source of motivation.

Jesus told a parable about forgiveness, concluding with the thought that "you should forgive your brother or sister from your heart." (See Matthew 18:35.) Think about what this idea means when you consider that "heart" refers to the subconscious mind. You can tell someone that you forgive them, but you can walk off and, in your mind, declare, "I don't forgive you." Jesus is saying, in effect, "When you've freed the offending person in your subconscious mind, then you've truly forgiven them." You're not just giving lip service to it, but you've forgiven them in the depths of your being.

Again, Jesus said, *Love the Lord your God with all your heart and with all your soul and with all your mind* (Matthew 22:37). Both the heart and the mind are mentioned here. We are meant to love God with all our conscious and subconscious thoughts and attitudes. In essence, we are to have our conscious and subconscious minds filled with the thoughts, words, nature, attributes, and characteristics of God. The Creator should be the "default mode" on our mental hard drives.

The beliefs and convictions of a leader regulate the nature of his leadership. You don't really believe something until it gets into your subconscious mind. Most of us can't break certain habits because we don't have the right thoughts and attitudes that will enable us to change. Your convictions determine what is stored in your heart, and your heart is the container of your attitudes. It's the bank you draw from that determines the way you live your life.

Thought: We are held accountable not only for our actions but also for our thoughts and attitudes.

Reading: Psalm 26:2

— DAY 41 —

ATTITUDE DEFINES LEADERSHIP

"David said to Saul, 'Let no one lose heart on account of this Philistine; your servant will go and fight him.'"
—1 Samuel 17:32

We are learning that the key to the spirit of leadership is not *ability*—it is *mentality*, or *attitude*. What you think is even more important than what you do.

What do I mean by "attitude"? Let me simply define attitude as "the mindset or mental conditioning that determines our interpretation of and response to our environments." It's our way of thinking. As we have discussed over the last several days, attitude is also a natural product of the integration of the self-worth, self-concept, self-esteem, and sense of value or significance that we derive from our Creator. In the above verse, when David confidently declares that he can defeat the giant Goliath, we see the attitude of leadership in action. In effect, your attitude is the manifestation of who you think you are. Leaders think about themselves in a distinct way, and this distinguishes them from followers.

Jesus, the great leadership trainer, said several times, *"Whoever has ears to hear, let them hear."* (See, for example, Mark 4:9; Luke 8:8.) Some people just want to listen; they don't want to hear, so important truths never get into their subconscious minds. The only way to get things into your subconscious mind is through repetition. You have to "download" them over a period of time. When you download something onto your computer, you need to wait until the download is finished before you can use it. You can't force it to download. It is the same with your heart. You must patiently allow the new information to settle into your subconscious.

Remember that leadership is both an aptitude and an attitude. No matter how much intellectual ability you have, if you don't have the right attitudes, your ability doesn't mean anything. Someone has said, "Attitude is a little thing that makes a big difference."[9]

Abraham Lincoln is a classic example of this. He failed to accomplish his goals many times, but he had an inner belief that he had something to offer his community, his state, and eventually his nation. This attitude of the heart was what kept him in the race even when he faced negative circumstances and setbacks. How do you react when you fail? You must have an inner belief that is stronger than your experience. Victor Frankl, a holocaust survivor, once said, "When we are no longer able to change a situation...we are challenged to change ourselves."[10]

Let us remember this foundational truth about leadership: no leader can rise above their attitude.

⌣⟶

Thought: When the attitude of the spirit of leadership is married to the ability of leadership in you, then you are a true leader.

Reading: 1 Samuel 17:26–50

---

9. Quoteresearch, "Attitude Is a Little Thing That Makes a Big Difference," Quote Investigator, March 13, 2013, https://quoteinvestigator.com/2013/03/13/attitude-little-big/.
10. Viktor E. Frankl, *Man's Search for Meaning* (Boston: Beacon Press, 2006), 112.

"ABOVE ALL ELSE, GUARD YOUR HEART"

"Above all else, guard your heart, for everything you do flows from it."   —Proverbs 4:23

When I mention the "heart," I imagine most people immediately think of the physical organ that beats in our chests. But that is not what this word means in the context of leadership. What is the heart? Scripture provides us with many truths about the heart. As we began to discuss earlier, when the Bible uses this word, it's usually referring to our subconscious minds and their contents.

From earliest writings, the heart has been a metaphor for the center of our being. The heart is the seat of our reasoning, the storehouse of all our thoughts, the seedbed for our ideas, and the center of our decision-making. It is the "hard drive" for our conscious minds. Our hearts or subconscious minds are what motivate us in our attitudes and actions, even though we may not be aware of what is influencing us.

Jesus gave much attention to this aspect of the human development and training process. He emphasized the following statements to His disciples:

> *For the mouth speaks what the heart is full of. A good man brings good things out of the good stored up in him, and an evil man brings evil things out of the evil stored up in him.*
> (Matthew 12:34–35)

> *But the things that come out of a person's mouth come from the heart, and these defile them. For out of the heart come evil thoughts—murder, adultery, sexual immorality, theft, false*

testimony, slander. These are what defile a person; but eating with unwashed hands does not defile them.

(Matthew 15:18–20)

In these simple statements, the principle of the heart and its power to control all of one's life is evident. According to Jesus, all our actions are motivated by the content of our hearts or what is stored in our subconscious minds.

In the book of Proverbs, we read, *"Let love and faithfulness never leave you; bind them around your neck, write them on the tablet of your heart"* (Proverbs 3:3). What is this *"tablet"* of the heart? The word refers to a polished board or plank that could be carved on and then read. What we *"write"* on our hearts we use as a reference for our attitudes and actions. Again, in Proverbs, we read, *"To humans belong the plans of the heart"* (Proverbs 16:1). The heart is where we sift things over and make decisions about what we want to do and be. Your entire life is controlled and determined by your heart. Therefore, you must guard it above all else.

Thought: The heart is the seat of our reasoning, the storehouse of all our thoughts, the seedbed for our ideas, and the center of our decision-making.

Reading: Philippians 4:7

— DAY 43 —

WHAT IS YOUR HEART ATTITUDE?

"Let the words of my mouth and the meditation of my heart be acceptable in Your sight, O LORD, my strength and my Redeemer." —Psalm 19:14 (NKJV)

The attitude of our hearts is so important that I want to summarize what we have been learning about it:

+ Your heart is the chamber that holds your convictions about all aspects of life.

+ Your convictions are your beliefs, and your beliefs generally originate from what you keep hearing and believe to be truth.

+ The heart is where all of what you have learned and repeatedly heard during your life is stored.

Your heart is also where all your culture is assimilated into your psyche. It is the center of your philosophy and the vantage point from which you view the world.

Since the heart stores what you truly believe, and your attitudes and actions are based on those beliefs, the heart or the subconscious mind is the *most vital component* in your relationship to life. This is why what you believe is essential—critical—to your life. Your beliefs better be right because you live out of your heart; you see through your heart; you interpret through your heart; you judge through your heart. Remember, Jesus warned His disciples about what was most important to them, saying, *"For where your treasure is, there your heart will be also"* (Matthew 6:21).

Developing the spirit of leadership means examining your heart and correcting what you have heard because much of what you have previously heard and accepted as truth has negatively influenced your image of yourself, your beliefs about your leadership potential, and your life decisions.

When we discover God's truth, and that truth is established in our subconscious minds, transformation will occur. This principle is the reason people can have what is called a "change of heart." They change their attitudes and beliefs, and this alters their actions and reactions. Are you receiving the right information? True leadership demands constant monitoring of what goes into the heart. If you discover the truth, then the truth will make you free. (See John 8:31–32.)

King Solomon wrote concerning the power of the heart, "As a face is reflected in water, so the heart reflects the real person" (Proverbs 27:19 NLT). The heart is the seat of life and determines the quality of our experiences in life and leadership. Leaders lead out of their hearts.

Thought: All our actions are motivated by the content of our heart.

Reading: Proverbs 3:5–6

— DAY 44 —

THE PURSUIT OF TRUTH

"You will know the truth, and the truth will set you free."
—John 8:32

One of the most famous questions of history is, "What is truth?" The most practical definition of truth I have discovered is "original information." A careful consideration of this definition reveals that the only one who knows the truth about something is the one who created it, for only the originator would have original information about their creation.

As recorded in John 8:32, Jesus said that the truth will make us free. Free from what? Free from error or false information. Jesus was therefore implying that whatever we learned before we received His information—God's truth—must be viewed with suspicion and, if necessary, deleted from our belief systems. If the source of your thoughts is not truth, then your thoughts are untrue or incorrect and your conclusions and beliefs are defective and contaminated—or will be soon. The result is a life lived in error and insecurity. What all this comes down to is that the most important pursuit in life is the pursuit of truth.

It is interesting to note that the Hebrew concept of knowledge or truth is "light," which implies that ignorance is "darkness." God Himself is described in the Bible as *"light; in him there is no darkness at all"* (1 John 1:5). Mankind without the original knowledge of itself from the Creator is like a lamp or a candle without a flame.

The book of Proverbs tells us that *"the spirit of a man is the lamp of the LORD, searching all the inner depths of his heart"* (Proverbs

20:27 NKJV). What happens when the light of that lamp goes out? It needs to be relit. It needs original knowledge—truth.

We read in the Psalms, "For You will light my lamp; The LORD my God will enlighten my darkness" (Psalm 18:28 NKJV). In other words, God will give the original knowledge, the truth, that we need, enlightening us and removing our ignorance. Jesus said, "No one lights a lamp and hides it in a clay jar or puts it under a bed. Instead, they put it on a stand, so that those who come in can see the light" (Luke 8:16). First the Creator enlightens us, and then we are to go out and influence others with the light that He has given us. True leadership is manifested when one individual uses their flame to light the lives of many others and help them discover the reservoir of hidden oil in their own lamps.

A statement Jesus made numerous times before He explained something was, "I tell you the truth." (See, for example, Matthew 6:2; Mark 9:41; Luke 18:17; John 8:51.) If you want to know the truth about yourself and the attitude you should have about yourself, you must listen to the words Jesus spoke about you. We need truth, and He is the source of it. He said, "I am the way and the truth and the life" (John 14:6). I believe He was saying, in essence, "I am the way to the truth that gives you life." Put another way, Jesus is the source of the truth that makes us come alive.

⁓

Thought: First the Creator enlightens us, and then we are to go out and influence others with the light that He has given us.

Reading: John 8:12–18

WHAT HAPPENED TO THE SPIRIT OF LEADERSHIP?

*"If the many died by the trespass of the one man [Adam],
how much more did God's grace and the gift that came by the
grace of the one man, Jesus Christ, overflow to the many!"*
—Romans 5:15

Now that we understand that God intended for men and women to walk in both *the leadership spirit* and *the spirit of leadership*, let's take a closer look at what occurred to humanity when God's plan was originally rejected. The fall of mankind, described in the second and third chapters of Genesis, records the great separation of human beings from their Source of creation. How did this separation happen?

For the protection of mankind, God had established natural laws that corresponded with humanity's nature and well-being. Instead of trusting that these parameters were established for their own good, human beings—consisting at that point of Adam and Eve—declared independence from their Source. Essentially, they thought that they could live apart from their Source and therefore severed their relationship with Him. Ultimately, what connected humanity to the Creator was His Spirit in us. After man disobeyed the laws of God, that Spirit departed, making the detachment complete. (See Genesis 2:5–9, 15–25; 3.)

When Adam and Eve cut themselves off from their Creator, they were in rebellion against their natural state. Their offense was basically a rejection of their true Source, and the natural and inevitable penalty of the offense was separation, or death. As in Adam and Eve's first rebellion, if we are cut off from the Source of our leadership spirit—when God's Spirit is absent from our lives—we are also cut off from the attitude and power that should flow from our leadership nature. We end up distorting the spirit of leadership instead of reflecting it in the light of our Source.

All the problems of mankind that we see today and have seen throughout our history stem from this act. When you declare independence from God, (1) you have to create your own identity, and (2) you become responsible for your own destiny. The problem is this: if you don't have the resources for living independently— that is, if you don't intrinsically have life in yourself—then your failure is inevitable.

The results of mankind's disconnection from its Source were devastating. Human beings lost their sense of identity and self-concept, as well as their sense of personal value and significance to themselves, their world, and the universe. Basically, man lost the knowledge of who he is, where he came from, what he is capable of, where he is going, and why he exists.

Although humans interrupted God's plan (instituted for their good), God had a restoration plan for the human race. This plan, effected by Jesus Christ, was to reconcile human beings to their Creator and enable them to receive His Holy Spirit again, thus reestablishing self-government within them so they could fulfill their God-given purposes. For that reason, to become a true leader, and to return to our original purpose, each of us needs to recognize the gift of God's grace given to us in Jesus Christ.

Thought: The human spirit can never know its leadership nature— its purpose, ability, potential, and power—without reconnecting with its Source.

Reading: Genesis 2:8–17

— DAY 46 —

THE NATURAL RESULT OF SEPARATION

*"But your iniquities have separated you from your God; your
sins have hidden his face from you, so that he will not hear."*
—Isaiah 59:2

We have established that what connects human beings to the
Creator is His Spirit in us. When mankind disconnected from
its Source by disobeying the laws of God, that Spirit departed,
making the detachment complete. The result was that we had no
direct way of relating to, communicating with, or receiving from
God. We lost both His power and the consciousness of the spirit
of leadership He had given us.

Everything the Creator made needs to remain connected to
its Source to fulfill its original purpose. Just as a plant dies when
it is detached from its source—the soil—or a fish dies when it is
detached from its source—the water—when a person is separated
from their source—the Spirit of God—then they, too, will naturally malfunction and die. If you're severed from your Source,
you're disconnected from the purpose of your creation. This is
what happened to the human race in the great separation.

Adam, as the first man, represented all of humanity. When
he declared independence from his Source, he detached not only
himself, but also all his future offspring, from true identity, purpose, protection, maintenance, preservation, productivity, meaning, and life. This is why God warned Adam ahead of time, saying,
in effect, "The day that you rebel against Me by disobeying My
command, you will surely die." (See Genesis 2:17.)

The concept of death here is not referring to the physical termination of the body. Rather, this death refers to the severing of the relationship man had with his Creator-Source. It refers to the demise of man's identity, sense of self-image, and self-worth. God was speaking of the spiritual death that comes from being cut off from Him. Moreover, just as the soil never kills a plant or the water never kills a fish when they are separated from their source, it is not the Creator who does the killing. He doesn't have to—death is a result, not an imposition. God's statement "You will surely die" is just the announcement of an outcome, not a threat. He didn't say, "The day you do this, I will kill you." He said, "You will surely die."

The loss of humanity's Source of purpose and power has led to a myriad of negative outcomes because of the confusion that inevitably resulted. The following questions have been asked by countless generations since Adam declared independence from his Source: "Who am I?" "Where am I from?" "Why am I here?" "What am I capable of doing?" "Where am I going?"

These five questions summarize the essence of the human struggle and are what I, over the years, have called the questions of the human heart. They control everything that each human being does and are the motivation for all human behavior. All our social, economic, spiritual, and relational activities spring from the pursuit of answers to these questions. Until they are answered satisfactorily, there can be no personal fulfillment, and life will have no meaning. These questions address the five most important discoveries in the human experience: identity, heritage, purpose, potential, and destiny. They are the heart of the leadership struggle, and when answered, they give birth to true leadership.

Thought: Everything the Creator made needs to remain connected to its Source to fulfill its original purpose.

Reading: Genesis 3:1–6

— DAY 47 —

LEADING WITHOUT CONNECTION

"No branch can bear fruit by itself; it must remain in the vine. Neither can you bear fruit unless you remain in me."
—John 15:4

Imagine that you have been walking along an isolated road for two days with no food or water, and the sun is blazing down on you. Suddenly, you notice a well in the distance. Even though you are tired, you run toward it with anticipation because you know that your thirst will be quenched. When you reach the well, however, you see a rope dangling over the opening, but no bucket. Deep down inside the well is what you need to satisfy your thirst and sustain your life, but you have no access to it.

This is a picture of the loss of the leadership spirit—of humanity being cut off from its life-giving Source. Always remember that the leadership spirit still exists deep down inside the makeup of every person because we are made in the image of our Creator. However, when we are not connected to Him, we can't fully manifest this gift in our lives because, just like the well without a bucket, we don't have the resources *to access it.* When we lose the Spirit of the Creator, we lose our *awareness* of both the leadership spirit as well as the *mindset* that enables us to exercise it effectively. This explains how humanity's lack of connection with the Spirit of the Creator has led to the loss of the spirit of leadership in the world.

One of my favorite analogies of the difference between the leadership spirit and the spirit of leadership is that of a computer's hardware versus its software. Simply put, the leadership spirit is the *inherent hardware,* and the spirit of leadership is the *necessary software* for the hardware to function. And God's Spirit is the Source that brings power to both.

Lacking the spirit of leadership is like buying a new computer that has all the hardware to enable you to run programs and carry out their functions, but then not having any power source to run the computer. Suppose, then, that you obtain a power source and plug it in. The computer hardware is turned on and ready to go, but you still need software for it to be of practical use to you. You have the knowledge of what the computer has been designed to do, and all the components of the hardware are ready for use. The potential is there, the ability is there, everything the manufacturer put into it is there, but it's almost as if you don't own a computer because you can't do anything with it.

This example illustrates the two-pronged nature of our problem of separation. First, even though our potential as leaders is still within us (the leadership spirit), we've lost our connection with our Source of purpose and power. Second, even when the connection with the Source is reinstated (when we receive God's Spirit again by salvation through Jesus Christ), unless we obtain the right "software"—that is, unless we recognize how a leader is meant to think and operate (the spirit of leadership)—we still won't be able to fulfill our potential. Our "hardware" and our "software" can be set up correctly only as we are connected to our Source by His Spirit *and* as we understand and act upon His truth and wisdom.

⌒

Thought: God's Spirit is the Source that brings power to both our "hardware" (leadership spirit) and our "software" (spirit of leadership).

Reading: John 15:1–5

— DAY 48 —

OUR INDWELLING POWER CONNECTION

"You...are in the realm of the Spirit, if indeed the Spirit of God lives in you." —Romans 8:9

I live in the Bahamas in an area known as the "hurricane zone." From time to time, we are subjected to the uncontrollable force of nature as the phenomena of the elements conspire to remind us of our vulnerability. Years ago, during hurricane season, when the massive hurricanes named Gene and Francis followed each other on a path right across our archipelago, I remember how helpless I felt. My wife and I made all our preparations and then sat waiting for the long-announced arrival of the category 4 and 5 storms. During one of the storms, the winds bore down on us like a living monster and shook the battened-down windows. At the height of the storm, the electricity went out, and we were left sitting in darkness.

I reached for the flashlight and surveyed the room. Then I took a walk through the darkened house and checked everything to make sure the shutters were holding. As I examined the rooms with the flashlight, I noticed the many items we had accumulated that had become so important to us, but that now were completely useless: the large-screen television, computers, printers, and other high-tech "toys" we had purchased.

I stood there in the dark for a moment and thought about all the power, potential, benefits, pleasure, and untapped functions trapped in each of these items that were completely useless and unbeneficial to me at that moment. They existed, but they could not contribute to my present situation and life. They were filled with possibility, but they could not deliver. Why? Because they were cut off from their source, their power supply. I then saw a true picture of mankind: a powerful creature full of divine potential, talents, gifts, abilities, untapped capacity, creativity, ingenuity, and productivity, who himself had been cut off from his power supply. If he doesn't reconnect with the Source, he will walk the earth living far below his intended privilege and capacity, victimized by his ignorance of both his Source and himself.

The Creator is passionately committed to our being reconnected to Him because (1) we are His beloved people, made in His image, and He doesn't want His image to be distorted or disgraced in the world, and (2) His purposes are permanent. He always accomplishes what He originally sets out to do. Despite humanity's declaring independence from its Source, the Creator hasn't changed His mind about His original purposes for us.

We were created to function attached to God; we can fulfill our true potential and maximize our full capacity only through this connection. The key to effective and successful living is the indwelling Spirit of God—called the Holy Spirit. The Holy Spirit, therefore, is the key to true leadership. The Spirit is the critical component in every human's existence because He is the power connection and the only hope for our rediscovering our true identity, self-image, self-worth, significance, self-esteem, and, ultimately, destiny.

Thought: The key to effective and successful living is the indwelling Spirit of God—called the Holy Spirit.

Reading: Romans 8:14–17

— DAY 49 —
GOD'S DIAGNOSIS

"You should no longer walk as the rest of the Gentiles walk, in the futility of their mind." —Ephesians 4:17 (NKJV)

When humanity lost the spirit of leadership, the result was spiritual, mental, and physical decline. Each consecutive generation since the fall of man has wandered farther and farther away from its leadership power. Human beings were disconnected from the Spirit of God, who had enabled them to know the mindset—the thoughts—of their Creator. They had no other place to get their thoughts from, so they got them from themselves and their environment. This is what man has been living on ever since: his own thoughts, the thoughts of his contemporaries, and the deceitfulness of his adversary—Satan. What a combination to build one's heart on!

God's diagnosis of man's condition is actually very different from what we usually think it is. It is not so much a religious problem as it is a *thought* problem. As Paul wrote, men and women walk *"in the futility of their mind"* (Ephesians 4:17 NKJV). Therefore, the Father sent Jesus Christ—the Word (God's thoughts)—to earth to correct and redirect our thinking. The apostle John wrote,

> *In the beginning was the Word, and the Word was with God, and the Word was God. He was with God in the beginning. Through him all things were made; without him nothing was made that has been made. In him was life, and that life was the light of all mankind. The light shines in the darkness, and the darkness has not overcome it.* (John 1:1–5)

The Greek word that is translated *"Word"* in this passage is *logos*, which means "The Divine Expression."[11] Jesus is God expressing Himself and His purposes to us. By sending us His Word, God sent us His thoughts and His original intent at creation. When someone is sick, and the doctor makes a diagnosis, the result of the diagnosis dictates the medication they prescribe. Therefore, God's prescription of sending His Word—His expressed thought in Jesus—indicates what He considered to be the source and cause of humanity's problem: a defective thought problem.

This is why, for three-and-a-half years, Jesus sat with His student-disciples—which included those businessmen who owned a fishing company, Peter, Andrew, James, and John—and challenged them to change their thinking by showing them the way a true leader thinks.

This shows us once more that, in the final analysis, our thinking creates our lives. Jesus came to give us back the original thoughts that we lost when we rebelled against our Source. When our *thoughts* are corrected, our *attitudes* will be transformed because our original thinking will be restored. This will ignite our spirit of leadership and enable us to fulfill our leadership potential.

Thought: When our thoughts are corrected, our attitudes will be transformed.

Reading: Ephesians 4:17–21

---

11. *Strong's*, #G3056.

— DAY 50 —

LIGHT THAT BRINGS FREEDOM

"The true light that gives light to everyone was coming into the world."   —John 1:9

A few years ago, I purchased a new laptop computer and was intrigued when I read through the operator's manual. All the usual information was there, but what caught my eye were the last few pages at the back of the booklet. These pages dealt with the warranty and guarantee issues and the stipulation concerning using only an authorized dealer. The principle was clear: the company honored only the work of an authorized dealer in regard to repairs, and any violation of this agreement would cancel the warranty.

When a manufacturer addresses the issue of repairing a problem with its product, it has its authorized dealers take care of the situation because they represent the manufacturer and are familiar with the product. The same principle holds true in the case of the fall of man from his relationship with his Creator, or Manufacturer. Our Manufacturer sent His one-and-only Authorized Dealer—Jesus Christ—to give us the original information about ourselves and to repair our damaged relationship with the Manufacturer. In its essence, the entire story of the Bible is about God—the Manufacturer—refitting His product—mankind—to accomplish His original purpose.

Jesus's assignment was to do everything necessary to reconnect mankind to his Source. Following our earlier analogy, Jesus came to restore power to the "computer"—He restored the Spirit of the Creator to our lives and gave us a new awareness of our purpose. Now we have the power to become what we were created to be.

Yesterday, we read, *"In the beginning was the Word,...and the Word was God"* (John 1:1). God sent Himself to give us the true information about ourselves. Again, Jesus said, *"You will know the truth [through the Word], and the truth will set you free"* (John 8:32). Through the Word, we are set free from all the misconceptions and falsehoods that resulted from our disconnection.

The apostle John wrote about Jesus as the life and light for every one of us: *"In him was life, and that life was the light [knowledge] of all mankind"* (John 1:4). Jesus came to bring life. You never really live until you get true information about yourself. *"The light [Jesus] shines in the darkness, and the darkness did not comprehend it"* (John 1:5 NKJV). As we shared earlier, darkness refers to ignorance, while light denotes knowledge. Jesus knows the truth about us—who we really are—and He is saying, "The more you know what I know about you, the more alive you will become."

"The true light that gives light to everyone was coming into the world" (John 1:9). Jesus knows the truth about every human being who is alive. That's why we go to Him for restoration. It is not to "get religion" but to rediscover our Source and our true selves.

The ultimate purpose of the suffering, death, and resurrection of Jesus Christ was to return the knowledge and power of the Creator to human beings so that we could fulfill God's original intent for us. Through Jesus's death, humanity could be fully reconnected and restored to God, and, as a result, the Spirit of the Creator was made available to people of every generation.

Thought: The more we know what God knows about us, the more alive we will become.

Reading: John 1

— DAY 51 —

RENEWING YOUR MIND

"Do not conform to the pattern of this world, but be transformed by the renewing of your mind." —Romans 12:2

Becoming reconnected to God is our salvation as human beings; however, it is just *the start* of our development into true leaders. The greatest challenge of those who have been reconnected with the Creator is having their attitude correspond with the mind of God's Spirit who now dwells within them. As we have discussed, Jesus has provided for the restoration of the Spirit in us, and when we receive that provision, we are spiritually reconnected to our Source; but the second step is that of *restoring the attitude of our minds* so that we can exercise our leadership spirit.

Being a leader is a natural part of our makeup, but *thinking* like a leader is not easy. Remember, embracing true leadership is a *process* not a *result*. Restoring the spirit of leadership requires a renewal of our thoughts and attitudes. We must transform our thoughts and align them with those that our Creator is thinking. Again, that is the reason the apostle Paul wrote to the church at Rome, *"Do not conform to the pattern of this world, but be transformed by the renewing of your mind. Then you will be able to test and approve what God's will is—his good, pleasing and perfect will"* (Romans 12:2).

Paul also wrote, *"Have the same mindset as Christ Jesus"* (Philippians 2:5), and *"Be made new in the attitude of your minds"* (Ephesians 4:23). He was talking to people who had already received God's Spirit, so he was indicating that they had not yet changed in the way they needed to. Just because we've been reconnected to our Source doesn't mean that we are thinking like Him in all ways. Our attitude needs to be adjusted.

The only way to have a transformed mind is to rediscover the revelation of the truth about yourself—the reality that you were created and designed to be a leader. You must internalize what God's Word says, His truth that leadership is your inherent nature, your purpose for existence, and your destiny. You must capture the essence of your purpose: You were born to rule—to lead. Once you capture this truth, then the transforming work begins.

The mental transformation—in our computer analogy, this would be the downloading of new software—is different from the initial reconnection. It is a process that takes time because it involves the changing of ingrained thoughts and habits. The vital difference is that now you have access to, and the power of, the Spirit of God, who will enable you to do this. Only when we are *made new in the attitude of* [our] *minds*" will we have the attitude that reflects the mind of the Spirit.

Thought: We must transform our thoughts and align them with those that our Creator is thinking.

Reading: Romans 12:1–2

—Day 52—

YOU ARE YOUR ATTITUDE

*"Be continually renewed in the spirit of your mind [having a
fresh, untarnished mental and spiritual attitude]."*
—Ephesians 4:23 (AMP)

Of all the aspects of the spirit of leadership, the power of attitude sits at the top. Attitude dictates your response to the present and determines the quality of your future. You are your attitude, and your attitude is you. If you do not control your attitude, it will control you.

Attitude creates your world and designs your destiny. It determines your success or failure in any venture in life. More opportunities have been lost, withheld, and forfeited because of attitude than from any other cause. Attitude is a more powerful distinction between people in life than beauty, power, title, or social status. It is more important than wealth—and it can keep you poor. It is the servant that can open the doors of life or close the gates of possibility. It can make beauty ugly and homeliness attractive. The distinguishing factor between a winner and a loser is attitude. The difference between a leader and a follower is attitude.

Again, I define attitude as "the mindset or mental conditioning that determines our interpretation of and response to our environments." It's our way of thinking.

We live our attitudes, and our attitudes create our lives. The story of the lion and the sheep that I related early in this devotional demonstrates the power of attitude. According to this illustration, if you believe in your heart that you are a sheep, then you will stay in the confines that others have placed you in or that you have made for yourself. If you believe that you are a lion, then you will venture beyond manmade limitations and embark on the life of leadership that you were born to live. You will develop into someone who inspires and influences others within your inherent domain.

No amount of training in leadership skills, courses in management methods, power titles, promotions, or associations can substitute for the right attitudes. As I wrote earlier, I am convinced that all the money in the world may make you rich, but it can never make you a leader. Your leadership development is determined by your perceptions of who you are and why you exist—in other words, your sense of significance to life.

To paraphrase Paul Meier, *attitudes are nothing more than habits of thought produced by your self-image, self-worth, and self-esteem, and habit can be acquired and changed by the reconditioning of the mind.*[12] Whatever your circumstances, you can experience the transformation of your outlook as you discover the attitudes that will enable you to be the leader that you were born to be.

⌒

Thought: Attitude creates your world and designs your destiny.

Reading: Philippians 4:13

---

12. Paul Meier's original quote is "Attitudes are nothing more than habits of thought, and habits can be acquired."

—DAY 53—
ATTITUDE IS LEARNED BEHAVIOR

"Whatever you have learned or received or heard from me, or seen in me—put it into practice." —Philippians 4:9

I had to learn the attitudes of true leadership at an early age. I was born in a very poor neighborhood in the Bahamas, in a wooden house on four stones. I had ten brothers and sisters, and I slept on the wooden floor of our two-bedroom house. I grew up in a neighborhood where there was poverty, and questionable characters were always present, exerting a negative influence.

Then, I went through a transformation. I desired to know the truth about my life and about life in general. During my teenage years, I questioned my disposition and challenged the status quo. The answers began to appear when I was given a Bible by my parents at age thirteen. I discovered in the pages of this book the amazing truth that I was created in the image of God and that His intent was for me to know Him and His will for my existence.

This discovery changed everything for me forever. When I began to read the Bible, I received new thoughts about myself and my world. Remember, the source of our thoughts is so important because our thoughts are the key to our quality of life. When I read the Bible, it contradicted what I was taught and what I saw with my eyes in the impoverished world around me. I began to believe what the Scriptures said rather than what I heard from outside sources, and that is how I developed a leadership mentality.

We change our attitudes by changing our beliefs, by changing our thoughts about everything in life—including ourselves. Someone has said, "What lies behind us and what lies before us are tiny matters compared to what lies within us."[13] The apostle John wrote, *"The one who is in you is greater than the one who is in the world"* (1 John 4:4).

I can't emphasize these words enough: the key to the spirit of leadership is attitude rather than aptitude. Remember, *it's not ability—it's mentality!*

We can change our attitudes. In fact, we are responsible for doing so. We cannot continue to function in a manner that we do not believe about ourselves. The day that we take responsibility for our attitudes is the day that we truly grow up.

Attitude determines everything. It is not enough to know the principles, precepts, and skills of leadership. We must cultivate the spirit of leadership by discovering and applying the attitudes of true leaders. Training in leadership really means training in attitude because attitude has to do with how we respond to life. We must think, talk, walk, dress, act, respond, decide, plan, work, relate, and live like leaders.

⌣

Thought: How you define yourself is the single most important statement you can make about yourself, and it is the heart of *attitude.*

Reading: 1 Timothy 4:6–11

---

13. Henry S. Haskins, "What Lies Behind Us and What Lies Before Us are Tiny Matters Compared to What Lies Within Us," Quote Investigator, January 11, 2011, https://quoteinvestigator.com/2011/01/11/what-lies-within/.

LEADERSHIP ATTITUDE #1: PURPOSE

"The purposes of a person's heart are deep waters, but one who has insight draws them out." —Proverbs 20:5

An attitude of *purpose* is the first attribute that separates followers from leaders. I cannot overemphasize how vital it is to understand the relationship between purpose and leadership. Remember, our true leadership cannot be manifested or maintained unless we have a sense of personal purpose. Purpose must always be considered because it is the discovery of a reason for one's existence, and it is defined as God's original intent for His creation. Every human being was created for a specific purpose, and when they discover and pursue that purpose, a leader is born.

Leaders don't just have jobs; they have lifetime assignments. Purpose creates a leader because it provides an assignment for life and signals a sense of significance. You must discover your purpose and the particular contribution you were destined to make to your generation. Remember, your leadership is hidden in your purpose, and your purpose is the key to your passion. No matter what position you may hold in life or in an organization, you must relate it to your sense of purpose and approach it with energy.

A leader is therefore someone who has a sense of personal purpose that gives them meaning and a reason for living, a strong sense of destiny and significance. Jesus's strong sense of destiny is reflected in His statements of purpose, such as these: *"For this cause I was born, and for this cause I have come into the world, that I should bear witness to the truth"* (John 18:37 NKJV). *"The Son of Man did not come to be served, but to serve, and to give his life as a ransom for many*" (Matthew 20:28). His purpose was His life's assignment.

In the lives of countless individuals, I have observed that when people discover who they were created to be, it starts a chain reaction toward fulfilling their leadership purpose. Remember the sequence: when you uncover a sense of meaning and purpose for your life, you become aware of your unique identity as a human being created in God's image. This identity provides the basis for your sense of personal value and worth as an individual. It contributes to a positive self-concept that gives you a spirit of confidence to move forward with your unique purpose, especially when you see your potential and begin to believe in your capacity to fulfill your purpose. When your confidence becomes a conviction about your ability to achieve that purpose, you gain a sense of destiny. These elements combine to motivate you to cultivate the gifts and talents the Creator has placed within you—including some that have been lying dormant inside you, waiting for you to understand your purpose and recognize your gifts.

It is at this point in the process that a leader becomes unstoppable. You have such a sense of your calling and assignment that you move ahead with your purpose despite obstacles, criticism, and setbacks.

Thought: Leaders don't just have jobs; they have lifetime assignments.

Reading: Luke 4:17–21

LEADERSHIP ATTITUDE #2: PASSION

"May he [God] give you the desire of your heart and make all your plans succeed."   —Psalm 20:4

An attitude of *passion* is the second most indispensable attribute of leadership and serves as the driving force of motivation that sustains the focus of the leader. Without passion, a leader lacks energy, and boredom begins to infect their mind and life. To become the leader that you were created to be, you must find a purpose for your life that produces a passion for living.

Every great man or woman became great because they possessed the spirit of passion. Yet I believe that this attitude is missing in 99 percent of the people of the world. This is why many are followers rather than leaders. Passion is rare in the human experience.

Why is passion so important? In the Psalms, we read, *"May he [God] give you the desire of your heart and make all your plans succeed"* (Psalm 20:4). Your plans will be successful if you truly desire to accomplish them. The word *desire* denotes not a casual interest in life but a deeply possessed drive for a desired end—a passion for a purpose. If you don't have a passion for something, you won't receive it. It's only when we have a passion for what we want to do that things start happening to enable us to fulfill it. Here is what passion accomplishes for us:

Passion motivates. When a leader is passionate about their purpose and vision, they do not need others to motivate them to work. They are their own motivation. Such a person is a self-starter. Ecclesiastes 9:10 says, *"Whatever your hand finds to do, do it with all your might."* One sign that you have come to understand your true purpose is that you possess a passion that motivates you.

Passion energizes. Someone who is doing what they were born to do is filled with energy and excitement. They can't wait to get out of bed in the morning. A leader's energy also gives them consistency. They don't stop working because of boredom or the myriad distractions they encounter daily. Working on their vision doesn't deplete their energy but only seems to fuel it.

Passion renews. Passion not only motivates and energizes, but it also renews the whole person. It satisfies the spirit because the person is fulfilling the Creator's purpose for them by doing what they were meant to do. It refreshes the soul because pursuing purpose and vision brings interest in life and hope for the future. It also often reinvigorates the body, giving people energy they never knew they had, relieving stress and tension, and sometimes even lessening or alleviating other physical symptoms.

Passion fortifies. Passion causes people to keep going regardless of obstacles because they are focused on fulfilling their purposes. In this way, it gives them resilience. Persistence and perseverance are essential because opposition and setbacks are part of the process of fulfilling vision.

~

Thought: Passion not only motivates and energizes, but it also renews the whole person.

Reading: Psalm 20:1–5

A DEEP CERTAINTY

"I know your deeds, that you are neither cold nor hot. I wish you were either one or the other!" —Revelation 3:15

Passion is a deep certainty that you need to do something. Your convictions have to do with your beliefs. Some people have no conviction about what they're doing, but a leader is a person of strong conviction. If you believe that you have discovered what you're supposed to do, this creates passion. Again, it makes you stand against and overcome opposition, resistance, criticism, and all other obstacles.

God likes people who are passionate. In Revelation 3:15–16, we read of His distaste for those who are lukewarm: *"I know your deeds, that you are neither cold nor hot. I wish you were either one or the other! So, because you are lukewarm—neither hot nor cold—I am about to spit you out of my mouth."* People who are satisfied with a lesser existence will never go where they need to be.

In contrast, a person with passion takes chances. They are not afraid to fail because they have a sense of destiny. They know that failure is an incident, but destiny is permanent. Leaders know that purpose is much bigger than one incident or several incidents. They keep on moving toward the fulfillment of their purposes no matter what.

Consider the following questions: How badly do you want something? Are you just existing, or are you pursuing a reason for living? Leaders don't just do, but they *feel* what they're doing. Their passion continually motivates and inspires them. Perhaps the average person just has a job; they put in their time and then go home.

Remember that true leaders don't just have jobs; they have lifetime assignments.

Leaders are those who have discovered something more important than life itself, and therefore:

+ Their passion is a source of determination.
+ Their passion overcomes resistance and pain.
+ Their passion is an incubator of courage.
+ Their passion is stronger than opposition and even death.

If you find that you are bored, then you have not yet discovered your purpose because passion is the driving force in life. Leadership is born when someone discovers their purpose for being and commits to pursue it at all costs.

Sow a thought, reap a belief.

Sow a belief, reap an attitude,

Sow an attitude, reap an action.

Sow an action, reap a habit.

Sow a habit, reap a character.

Sow a character, reap a destiny.

Thought: Passion is a deep certainty that you need to do something.

Reading: Revelation 3:14–20

—DAY 57—

PASSION REVEALS DESTINY

"For I know the plans I have for you," declares the Lord, *"plans to prosper you and not to harm you, plans to give you hope and a future."* —Jeremiah 29:11

Throughout the Bible, God declares that He has a plan and purpose for our lives. Therefore, our passion also comes from our sense of destiny. If you become distracted, or opposition stands in your way, your destiny still pulls you in the direction of your desire because you can't imagine not fulfilling it.

Passion comes from something outside this world and is connected to it. As long as you're living for something only on earth, your passion won't last. It must be connected to something that is bigger than your own existence. If you get your passion from something on earth, then when it stops, you will stop. Instead, if you capture a sense of a destiny that existed before you were born and will continue to exist after you pass from this earth—if you feel you're involved in something that is larger than yourself—then you're on your way to leadership. Passion is born when you connect to both the past and the future.

Passion is also ignited by a revelation of the future—where you want to go with your life. When the Creator's vision for you is so vivid that you can see it in your mind's eye, this picture creates a passion to arrive there. Many people will criticize your passion because they don't see what you see. A leader usually moves toward things that can't yet be seen but will be manifested in the future.

When you understand that the Creator's providential hand is on your life, then you know that you are not just an experiment but part of a larger program, orchestrated by God, and that you have a specific role to play. This understanding of His providence causes your passion to come alive. In Jeremiah, God spoke of His providence toward His people:

> *"For I know the plans I have for you," declares the Lord, "plans to prosper you and not to harm you, plans to give you hope and a future. Then you will call on me and come and pray to me, and I will listen to you. You will seek me and find me when you seek me with all your heart."*
>
> (Jeremiah 29:11–13)

A person with passion, therefore, has a deep resolution in their soul and is determined to accomplish what they were born to do. This is not for their own sake alone, but also for the sake of others who will be blessed through the fulfillment of their purpose.

You're not living just for yourself anymore but for all those in the past and future to whom you're tied through a common purpose. Again, a true leader always thinks in terms of both yesterday and tomorrow—they build *on* the past, and they build *for* the future.

Thought: A leader usually moves toward things that can't yet be seen but will be manifested in the future.

Reading: Numbers 23:19

—DAY 58—

LEADERSHIP ATTITUDE #3: INITIATIVE

"I press toward the mark for the prize of the high calling of God in Christ Jesus." —Philippians 3:14 (KJV)

An attitude of initiative is the third attribute of true leaders that distinguishes them from perpetual followers. They don't wait for others to do what they know they should or could do. Leaders don't wait for the future to come; they create it. The apostle Paul declared, *"This one thing I do, forgetting those things which are behind, and reaching forth unto those things which are before, I press toward the mark for the prize of the high calling of God in Christ Jesus"* (Philippians 3:13–14 KJV).

This attitude of initiative makes the difference between a plan and an actual result. In other words, vision is a desire, while initiative gets it accomplished.

Let's look at some descriptions of initiative and initiators:

+ Initiative is a catalyst.

+ Initiative is taking action.

+ Initiative springs from self-motivation.

+ Initiators are self-starters who don't need outside urging to do something.

+ Initiators make specific decisions to begin things.

The Creator is our primary example of what it means to have the leadership attitude of initiative. The account of creation in the book of Genesis starts with, *"In the beginning God created the heavens and the earth. Now the earth was formless and empty, darkness was over the surface of the deep, and the Spirit of God was hovering* over the waters. And God said, 'Let there be light,' and there was light" (Genesis 1:1–3).

Before God spoke, the earth was formless, empty, and dark. It would have remained that way if He hadn't initiated the process of creation. He saw the earth's potential and transformed it into something that had form, was teeming with created beings, and was filled with light. The most important lesson here is hidden in the words *"In the beginning God created."* Here we see that the spirit of leadership initiates activity and activates change. Leaders don't just dream; they awaken and act on their dreams.

Leaders utilize the power of initiative because they:

+ Believe in the integrity and faithfulness of their Creator
+ Believe in their causes
+ Believe in their competence
+ Are not afraid to fail

To become the leader that you were born to be, you must cultivate the spirit of initiative. Don't wait for others to do what you know you could and should do. Be a leader—*initiate*.

Thought: Leaders don't wait for the future to come; they create it.

Reading: 1 Timothy 6:11–12

— Day 59 —

SIX PRINCIPLES OF INITIATIVE

"Whatever you do, work at it with all your heart, as working for the Lord, not for human masters." —Colossians 3:23

I have identified six principles of initiative that will help you to develop this attitude of the spirit of leadership:

1. Initiative is the key to accomplishment.

There are numerous examples of inventors, composers, and others who initiated works out of their imaginations that otherwise would have remained mere potential. Consider what ideas and desires you want to bring to reality and how taking initiative would be the catalyst for their manifestation.

2. Initiative is the power of momentum.

Inertia is a fact of life. *Merriam-Webster.com Dictionary* describes *inertia* as an "indisposition to motion, exertion, or change."[14] Things don't get started, progress, or get back on track once they've stalled unless someone takes action to set them on the right course again. At a baseball game, a base coach urges the runners to round the bases and make it to home plate before they are thrown out. He helps them to keep their momentum. Similarly, the attitude of initiative enables you to be your own coach so that you maintain momentum in pursuit of your life's purpose.

3. Initiative is the manifestation of decision.

Nothing can be accomplished unless a decision has been made concerning it. In our everyday lives, we don't buy a house, choose a

---

14. *Merriam-Webster.com Dictionary*, s.v. "inertia," https://www.merriam-webster.com/dictionary/inertia.

jacket, or select one form of insurance over another unless we specifically decide to take one thing and put aside all other options. This principle holds true as we exercise our gift of leadership. Initiative enables us to make choices that help us to move forward in our goals.

4. Initiative is the manifestation of confidence and faith.

We often hesitate to take initiative because we are afraid of responsibility or of the consequences of our actions. Yet the writer of Hebrews quoted this statement of the Lord: *"But my righteous one will live by faith. And I take no pleasure in the one who shrinks back"* (Hebrews 10:38). When we exhibit the attitude of initiative, it shows that we are operating in faith and the confidence that God will see us through as we pursue the purposes that He has for us.

5. Initiative is the spirit of creativity.

Inventors have the habit of doing multiple experiments. They keep trying until something works. Initiative often works in a similar way. A willingness to keep starting and attempting things as we pursue our purposes sparks the spirit of creativity and yields good results for those who delight in trying "one more thing."

6. Initiative is the key to obedience.

When we know that we're supposed to do something, that is when we should begin to do it. Holding back until we feel like it or until the circumstances are better is not conducive to the practice of doing what we need to do in order to accomplish our goals.

⌒

Thought: When we exhibit the attitude of initiative, it shows that we are operating in faith.

Reading: Colossians 3:23–24

—Day 60—

A WILLINGNESS TO WALK ALONE

"But Jesus often withdrew to lonely places and prayed."
—Luke 5:16

Sometimes initiative requires a *willingness to walk alone* as you pursue your purpose. Ask yourself: "How do I react when people oppose me or disregard my ideas? Do I immediately give up on my plans? Or am I willing to keep pursuing my dream because I am convinced of my purpose and because my passion for my vision won't allow me to discard it?"

Because leaders do not seek popularity, and because their visions are usually innovative and counter to the status quo, they often have to walk alone—especially at first. But those who practice leadership are willing to walk alone until the crowd catches up. Jesus Christ frequently had to walk alone as He moved toward the fulfillment of His purpose of redeeming the world. If you must walk alone, draw strength from the One who walked alone in His vision in order to reconcile you to your Creator.

> *Fixing our eyes on Jesus, the pioneer and perfecter of faith. For the joy set before him he endured the cross, scorning its shame, and sat down at the right hand of the throne of God. Consider him who endured such opposition from sinners, so that you will not grow weary and lose heart.* (Hebrews 12:2–3)

Leaders not only must be able to *walk alone* at times, but they also need to be able to *stand alone*. The demands of leadership may require that you stand alone in the face of conflict, public opinion, or crisis. Are you willing to stand alone for the truth and for correct principles, staying committed to your purpose? Jesus was forsaken by all His disciples in His greatest hour of need, yet He stood firm and saw His purpose fulfilled. (See, for example, Mark 14:43–51.) Paul, too, was abandoned by coworkers and friends in his ministry amid the pressures of persecution and hardship, yet he kept going. (See, for example, 2 Timothy 4:16–17.)

Sometimes, for short periods, a leader even needs to *choose to be alone*. Because of the weight of their task, they must take time to be by themselves in order to process their responsibilities; renew their spirit, mind, and body; and receive guidance from God. Luke the physician wrote about Jesus, "*The news about him spread all the more, so that crowds of people came to hear him and to be healed of their sicknesses. But Jesus often withdrew to lonely places and prayed*" (Luke 5:15–16). Do you have the capacity to pull away from the crowd so you can gain perspective and hear from God?

⌣

Thought: Leaders must be able to *walk alone*, *stand alone*, and *be alone*.

Readings: Hebrews 4:14–16; Luke 5:12–16

—Day 61—

LEADERSHIP ATTITUDE #4: PRIORITIES

"Let your eyes look straight ahead; fix your gaze directly before you."   —Proverbs 4:25

The attitude of *priorities* is the fourth important attribute of leadership. Any activities that we undertake inevitably consume our time, talents, effort, energy, and life. What we do, therefore, determines who we are and what we become. All true leaders are distinguished by their strong sense of priorities. They are always clear about what is important to them and desire to attend to the principal issue at hand. The key to this ability is applying the attitude of priority.

What is priority? Let's begin with some definitions. A priority is (1) something that has a prior claim on us; (2) something that merits our primary attention; (3) something that receives our primary resources; (4) something that has a right to supersede other things.

Effective leadership involves the management of your priorities. True leaders have learned how to distinguish between what is truly important for their lives and the fulfillment of their purposes and what is an urgent but temporary need. They have also discovered how to distinguish between options that are good and ones that are best for them. Because of these things, they have narrow agendas and short to-do lists.

How do we determine what is really important in our lives? We find a valuable guideline in a statement by Paul in his first letter to the Corinthians: *"Everything is permissible for me, but not all things are beneficial. Everything is permissible for me, but I will not* be enslaved by anything [and brought under its power, allowing it to control me]" (1 Corinthians 6:12 AMP).

We live in an age when, particularly in the United States, Great Britain, and the European Union, people have a myriad of choices regarding their lifestyles, careers, and leisure time. We can do many things, but not everything is constructive to our lives. One of our major responsibilities as leaders is determining what is best for us according to our life's purpose and vision. Paul knew about being single-minded in the pursuit of a purpose when he wrote this statement, which we considered earlier: "I press on toward the goal to win the prize for which God has called me heavenward in Christ Jesus" (Philippians 3:14).

Thus, true leaders must distinguish between what is good, which may be a variety of things, and what is right—good things that are specifically suited to their purpose. Leadership always has a narrow agenda and a concentrated to-do list. Leadership must never get bogged down in details but should always allow the priorities of the vision to set the agenda.

The greatest leader of all time, Jesus Christ, spoke about the importance of priorities, saying, "But seek first the kingdom of God and His righteousness, and all these things shall be added to you" (Matthew 6:33 NKJV). If you want to experience maximum living, it is important to narrow your life's priorities to the few that are the best for you according to your purpose.

⌒

Thought: True leaders have a clear sense of what they need to do.

Reading: Proverbs 4:25–27

CULTIVATE THE ART OF PRIORITY

"For in him [God] we live and move and have our being."
—Acts 17:28

As true leaders, our first priority is a clear and open relationship with God our Source. He is the Author of our lives and the Initiator of our visions, and we must endeavor always to maintain a vital connection with Him through His Son Jesus Christ.

Jesus answered, "I am the way and the truth and the life. No one comes to the Father except through me. If you really know me, you will know my Father as well. From now on, you do know him and have seen him." (John 14:6–7)

Our second priority is our relationships with our family members. The pursuit of our visions should not cause us to overlook our families. Paul wrote, *"Anyone who does not provide for their relatives, and especially for their own household, has denied the faith and is worse than an unbeliever"* (1 Timothy 5:8). Because leadership demands the giving of oneself to others, no leader's time is fully their own. Their gifts, talents, and experiences are employed in service to others. Leaders belong to their generations and not to themselves. This has a direct effect on their families, close friends, and others dear to them.

Jesus found Himself in this situation at the age of twelve when, after staying behind in Jerusalem to speak with the teachers in the temple, He had to say to His earthly parents, *"Why were you searching for me?... Didn't you know I had to be in my Father's house?"* (Luke 2:49). Yet, He always respected Mary and Joseph: *"They did* not understand what he was saying to them. Then he went down to Nazareth with them and was obedient to them" (verses 50–51).

Your family's needs are not negated by the needs of your vision. As you seek God and make plans for carrying out your purpose, make sure you have not neglected your most important responsibility next to God. The leader must be careful to strike a balance between serving people and meeting his family responsibilities and other obligations.

Perhaps it's time to ask yourself, "How do my current priorities line up with God's purposes for my life?" Think through your present priorities. Perhaps you haven't really established any priorities at all and are living in crisis mode. Whatever seems most pressing at the time gets your attention.

To become the leader that you were created to be, you must cultivate the art of priority—choosing and distinguishing between what is important and what is urgent. Leadership means knowing the difference between busyness and effectiveness. Again, true leaders distinguish between an opportunity and a distraction, and between what is good for them and what is right for them. Leaders know that priorities protect their valuable energy, time, resources, and talents.

Thought: How do my current priorities line up with God's purposes for my life?

Reading: Acts 17:24–28

— Day 63 —

LEADERSHIP ATTITUDE #5: GOAL-SETTING

"Many are the plans in a person's heart, but it is the Lord's purpose that prevails." —Proverbs 19:21

All true leaders possess attitude number five: *goal-setting*, which includes being goal-driven. Leaders distinguish themselves from followers by their commitment to preestablished goals. They regulate their activities and measure their progress against prescribed objectives and milestones.

Everyone in the world is a goal-setter, in one way or another. Many times, we don't realize that we are setting goals, but whenever we make plans to shop at a grocery store, go to school, do the laundry, or meet friends for a meal, we are in reality setting goals.

Even those who are failing at life are setting goals that cause them to fail. In fact, many of us plan *not* to do things that would make us successful. When we don't achieve what we want to achieve or accomplish what we desire to accomplish, the problem is not goal-setting, in itself. Instead, it's that we don't set goals for the things we truly care about, or we set the wrong kind of goals. A leader understands how to set the right goals. This is a vital attitude to cultivate because your future and your life depend on the goals you set—either consciously or subconsciously. Where you end up in life is a result of the goals that you set or did not set for your life.

What should determine the goals that we set and the plans that we make? Again, it is our purpose and vision in life. Success comes from the discipline of goal-setting according to one's purpose.

What is the relationship between purpose and plans? The book of Proverbs says, *"Many are the plans in a person's heart, but it is the LORD's purpose that prevails"* (Proverbs 19:21). According to the wisdom of this statement, we can understand three things about the relationship between purpose and plans (goal-setting): (1) Purpose *precedes* plans because the Creator established our purposes even before we were born. (2) Purpose is *more important than* plans. (3) Purpose is *more powerful than* plans.

We have to know our purpose and focus on it before we can begin planning, because plans that don't get us to our purpose are counterproductive. Purpose is God's original intent for you. Therefore, you need to know your destination so that you can set your goals.

Goals also protect us from the undue influence of other people. True leaders are always zealous for and jealous of their goals because these goals represent their lives. When our goals change, our lives change, so we must carefully guard our goals.

If you don't have any goals, other people will run your life. Solomon, the great king of Israel, declared, *"Whoever has no rule over his own spirit is like a city broken down, without walls"* (Proverbs 25:28 NKJV). If nothing controls and orders your life, then you are open season for other people, and you won't accomplish your purpose. Also, remember that the more successful you become, the more people will compete for your time, so you will have to guard your goals even more carefully.

~~~~~

Thought: If you think you can do it, that's confidence; if you *do* it, that's competence.

Reading: 1 Corinthians 9:24

— Day 64 —

THE POWER OF GOALS

"Suppose one of you wants to build a tower. Won't you first sit down and estimate the cost to see if you have enough money to complete it?" —Luke 14:28

Once you know your purpose, you begin to understand the power of goals for fulfilling that purpose. What is a goal? A goal is a prerequisite for the attainment of an ultimate plan. A goal is an established point for achievement that leads to a greater accomplishment. It is also a point of measure for progress toward an ultimate purpose.

In the book of Luke, Jesus cautioned the crowds about counting the cost when setting out to do something. On this occasion, He was speaking about the decision to become one of His followers: *"Suppose one of you wants to build a tower. Won't you first sit down and estimate the cost to see if you have enough money to complete it? For if you lay the foundation and are not able to finish it, everyone who sees it will ridicule you, saying, 'This person began to build and wasn't able to finish'"* (Luke 14:28–30).

Goals give us a structure for accomplishing our plans one step at a time. They give us a starting place and an ending place, and they help us to focus. Here are some of the benefits of goals:

+ Goals separate achievers from dreamers.
+ Goal-setting is the art of discipline.
+ Goals give specifics to the plan.
+ Goals create targets for our energy.
+ Goals protect us from procrastination.

It is helpful to have some guidelines for the development and recording of our goals because, otherwise, we can easily lose sight of them and their relationship to our purposes:

- Goals must relate to our ultimate purpose.
- Goals must be defined in a clear and simple way.
- Goals must be written.
- Goals must be visual.
- Goals must be measurable.
- Goals must be flexible.

Finally, true leaders understand the nature and value of goals and how their lives are influenced by them. This is why leaders have the following relationship with their goals:

- Leaders communicate their goals.
- Leaders are committed to their goals.
- Leaders are disciplined by their goals.
- Leaders believe in their goals.
- Leaders focus on their goals.
- Leaders measure their progress and success by their goals.
- Leaders revise their goals when necessary.
- Leaders protect their goals from interference.
- Leaders transfer their goals to their coworkers and to the next generation.

If you want to be successful as a leader in your domain, set goals for your life!

Thought: The secret to leadership success is living a focused life in line with your purpose. Goals give us a structure for accomplishing our plans one step at a time.

Reading: James 2:14–26

— Day 65 —

LEADERSHIP ATTITUDE #6: TEAMWORK

"From [Christ] the whole body, joined and held together by every supporting ligament, grows and builds itself up in love, as each part does its work." —Ephesians 4:16

The attitude of teamwork is the sixth important attribute of leadership. Henry Ford once said, "Coming together is a beginning. Keeping together is progress. Working together is success."[15]

True leaders possess the attitude of teamwork because they do not care who gets the credit. They move people from their personal and private goals to serving the needs of the common good. A team spirit manifests the difference between ambition and the pursuit of a God-given destiny. Ambition is a private thing that you want to do only for your own benefit, whereas destiny is a big picture that involves benefiting others. Ralph Waldo Emerson said, "There is no limit to what can be accomplished if it doesn't matter who gets the credit."[16]

A leader is always a team player. True leaders are continually cognizant of the fact that no great accomplishment has ever been achieved by one individual alone. This is a practical principle, but its reality is also by design. The apostle Paul wrote to the Ephesian church:

Speaking the truth in love, we will grow to become in every respect the mature body of him who is the head, that is, Christ.

15. Henry Ford, "Quotes," Goodreads, https://www.goodreads.com/quotes/118854-coming-together-is-the-beginning-keeping-together-is-progress-working.
16. Ralph Waldo Emerson, "Quotes," Goodreads, https://www.goodreads.com/quotes/519851-there-is-no-limit-to-what-can-be-accomplished-if.

From him the whole body, joined and held together by every supporting ligament, grows and builds itself up in love, as each part does its work. (Ephesians 4:15–16)

Mankind was created so that people would benefit from one another's mutual contributions as they live and work together. This is so they will not become self-centered, will learn to care for the needs of others, and will be able to multiply the reach of their gifts by combining their talents as they create and produce things. After all, God Himself, though He is one unified Spirit being, expresses His creative activity through the divine teamwork of Father, Son, and Holy Spirit.

A leader understands that every person was created to fill a need. Everyone has an ability that no one else has and is indispensable in the world. Likewise, because of their unique gifts and perspectives, each human being is a solution to a certain problem that needs to be solved.

A team player has a humble spirit and recognizes that they have both strengths and weaknesses and need the strengths of others to support them where they are weak. To become the leader that you were created to be, you must embrace and encourage the unique gifts, abilities, differences, and value that each team member brings to the whole. Leadership success is measured by how much work one can accomplish through the team.

⌒

Thought: Mankind was created so that people would benefit from one another's mutual contributions as they live and work together.

Reading: Ephesians 4:11–16

FOUR PRINCIPLES OF TEAMWORK

"So in Christ we, though many, form one body, and each member belongs to all the others." —Romans 12:5

Teamwork is defined as the ability to work together toward a common vision. Because it directs individual accomplishment toward organizational objectives, teamwork is the fuel that allows common people to attain uncommon results. Let's look at some principles of teamwork:

1. *Partnership is the Creator's idea.* When the Creator first brought mankind into the world, He had the idea of partnership in mind: *"The Lord God said, 'It is not good for the man to be alone. I will make a helper suitable for him'"* (Genesis 2:18).

2. *Teamwork is necessary for the fulfillment of purpose.* Remember, at creation, God said, *"Let Us make man in Our image, according to Our likeness; let **them** have dominion"* (Genesis 1:26 NKJV). The mandate of dominion over the earth, which requires the spirit of leadership, was given to both males and females. This means that teamwork is a built-in requirement for the fulfillment of our purposes in the world.

3. *Teamwork is the Creator's plan for leadership.* While God often calls individuals to carry out His purposes, He doesn't want them to pursue their callings alone. Even Moses, who was called the friend of God and did extraordinary things, needed leadership help. In the book of the prophet Micah, God said, *"I sent Moses to lead you, also Aaron and Miriam"* (Micah 6:4). Moses did not rule alone but was given the help of his brother and sister. And at a time when Moses tried to take on too much responsibility, his

father-in-law reminded him that he needed to delegate responsibility, or the work would be too much for him. (See Exodus 18:7–26.) We also see the idea of teamwork in the first-century church with the traveling teams of Paul and Barnabas, Peter and John, and Priscilla and Aquila. When Paul worked with the churches he founded, he often had many coworkers who assisted him.

4. *Teamwork was emphasized by Jesus.* Jesus Himself did not carry out His ministry alone but instead gathered a group of twelve primary disciples to assist Him and learn from His example. When He sent out these disciples to minister, He told them to go two by two. (See Mark 6:7.)

There are many benefits of teamwork. Once more, teamwork intrinsically appreciates the diversity of gifts that the team members bring to the partnership or group. Paul wrote, *"Just as each of us has one body with many members, and these members do not all have the same function, so in Christ we, though many, form one body, and each member belongs to all the others. We have different gifts, according to the grace given to each of us"* (Romans 12:4–6).

The spirit of teamwork offers the following benefits: (1) Teamwork gives opportunity for participation. (2) Teamwork provides the environment for people's talents and gifts to be released. (3) Teamwork gives both personal and corporate satisfaction. (4) Teamwork recognizes the value of each part/person.

Thought: Teamwork provides the environment for people's talents and gifts to be released.

Reading: Romans 12:3–8

LEADERSHIP ATTITUDE #7: INNOVATION

"Sing to the LORD *a new song; sing to the* LORD*, all the earth."*   —Psalm 96:1

The spirit of true leadership is always manifested in attitude number seven: *innovation.* Innovation is the creative reserve of true leaders. The very nature of leading demands an innovative spirit as a leader takes followers to an as-yet undiscovered world of vision.

The ultimate goal of leadership is to successfully accomplish a predetermined vision to fulfill a primary purpose. The role of the leader is to provide a sense of purpose, vision, motivation, and momentum, as well as a productive environment in which to accomplish the task. A key quality of leadership in this regard is an innovative and creative mindset.

One of the principal characteristics of effective leaders is their ability to think outside the box. True leaders learn from their experiences, but they never live in them. They never live their lives by prior experiences, or else they would become entrenched in the past. Leaders don't allow the past to dictate or entrap the future. They possess the capacity to combine old ideas and concepts in order to create new ones. They never believe that there is only one way to accomplish any task. Therefore, they are not prisoners of tradition.

In light of the mindset of the innovator, let's look at some definitions of innovation. Innovation is:

- The capacity to create new approaches and concepts to deal with old and new challenges

- The perceptivity to see possibilities in the combination of old and new concepts
- The creation, development, and application of untested ways of solving old and new problems
- The capacity to think beyond the known, defy the norm, and believe in one's abilities to solve problems

Our ability to innovate comes from the fact that we are made in the image and likeness of God, who has an innovative spirit. The apostle Paul wrote that we are to *"put on the new self, which is being renewed in knowledge in the image of its Creator"* (Colossians 3:10). This means that the more we are transformed into the image of the One who created us, the more innovative we will become.

An examination of the attitudes and actions of the Creator's innovative spirit leads us to the following conclusions: The Creator created with diversity. He never repeated anything in creation, never did the same miracle twice in the same way, never believed anything was impossible, never dealt with humanity according to its norms and expectations, always solved problems in unexpected and untraditional ways, and challenged humanity to think beyond its current experience.

Thought: Innovation is the creative reserve of true leaders.

Reading: Exodus 35:30–35

—Day 68—

JESUS THE INNOVATOR

"The blind receive sight, the lame walk, those who have leprosy are cleansed, the deaf hear, the dead are raised, and the good news is proclaimed to the poor."   —Matthew 11:5

In reading the New Testament, we discover that Jesus is the greatest example of the leadership spirit of innovation. During His time on earth over two thousand years ago, He demonstrated the same innovative spirit as the heavenly Father. His creativity was manifested in all His work among people. In performing His miracles, He never repeated any single method but always used a different approach to solve each problem.

For example, Jesus healed the blind using several different methods. For some, He merely touched their eyes, and they were made well. For one, He laid His hands on the man's eyes and put mud on them, and then laid His hands on them again to cause him to receive his sight. For still another, He simply spoke the words, *"Go, your faith has healed you,"* and the person was healed. (See Matthew 9:27–30; Matthew 20:30–34; Mark 8:22–25; Mark 10:46–52.)

When Jesus wanted to feed thousands of people who had gathered to hear Him speak, He didn't have His disciples buy food at the market; instead, He multiplied five loaves and two fish so that everyone was well fed, and He had leftovers to spare. (See, for example, Matthew 14:14–21.) When Jesus raised the dead, He did so in distinct ways. One time, He touched a young man's coffin and then told the man to get up; in another instance, He took a little girl by the hand and told her to get up; and at another point,

He called out to Lazarus, who was still in his grave, and Lazarus walked out of the tomb alive. (See Luke 7:11–15; Mark 5:35–42; John 11:38–44.)

In a final example, one time when Jesus and His disciples needed to pay taxes, and Peter was concerned about it, Jesus told him to go fishing and that the first fish he caught would have money inside its mouth that they could use to pay the taxes. (See Matthew 17:24–27.) Jesus's leadership style shows that true leadership demands that we always consider new ways to solve old problems.

Having a predetermined mindset hinders the leadership spirit of innovation. In the book of the prophet Isaiah, God said, *"Forget the former things; do not dwell on the past. See, I am doing a new thing! Now it springs up; do you not perceive it?"* (Isaiah 43:18–19). Whenever you encounter a project, a challenge, or a problem, practice thinking in new ways and with a different mindset. Ask the Creator to give you a fresh perspective, and see what happens!

Leaders don't follow paths—they create trails. They venture where others don't dare to tread. Know that the horizon of life offers great opportunities. Leaders take time to sit and think of things that have not yet been done and then make plans to get them done. Venture into the uncomfortable zone—*innovate.*

⌒

Thought: Harness creativity and explore the uncharted worlds of the untested.

Reading: Ephesians 3:20

— DAY 69 —
LEADERSHIP ATTITUDE #8:
ACCOUNTABILITY

"Have the same mindset as Christ Jesus: who, being in very nature God, did not consider equality with God something to be used to his own advantage." —Philippians 2:5–6

The eighth attitude of leaders is *accountability*. The spirit of leadership always possesses a sense of being accountable and responsible to others. What is accountability? In a nutshell, accountability is giving a reckoning for one's conduct and reporting on one's progress. It is also an admission of motives and reasons for taking certain actions.

True leaders readily embrace submission to authority and are conscious of their stewardship of the trust given to them by those whom they serve. The spirit of leadership seeks to be faithful to this sacred trust of the followers rather than doing only what will please the leader.

Leaders are at risk of falling into a particular danger, and submission to authority helps to prevent this from happening. Remember, the key to good leadership is the power to influence through inspiration, not manipulation. The potential danger of leaders is that they will wield power without answering to anyone else for their actions. Dictatorship and tyranny occur when a leader fails to submit to authority. The protection of leadership, therefore, is in *voluntary submission to a trusted authority*. The spirit of accountability is the active manifestation of submission to such authority.

Let's clarify to whom a leader must be accountable:

1. Himself or herself (their conscience)
2. The primary stakeholders
3. The general family of humanity
4. The Creator, as the ultimate authority

All true leaders are aware of their responsibility to higher authority. Particularly in relation to the Creator, they are aware that they are accountable before God for their words and actions. Remember, each person is meant to fulfill their unique part in the whole, each being responsible for leadership in their sphere of assignment and responsible ultimately to God. Each of us was created to be a leader led by God's Spirit, and no one is to lord it over others or prevent them from maximizing their potential.

In addition, a true leader is always conscious that they are not a law unto themselves but should uphold established laws and treat others with respect as people made in the image and likeness of the Creator. They also listen to the advice and input of credible authority.

Perhaps the best advice for being accountable is what Paul wrote to the first-century church at Colossae: *"Whatever you do, work at it with all your heart, as working for the Lord, not for human masters, since you know that you will receive an inheritance from the Lord as a reward. It is the Lord Christ you are serving"* (Colossians 3:23–24).

Thought: All true leaders are aware of their responsibility to a higher authority.

Reading: Philippians 2:1–11

—Day 70—

JESUS WAS ACCOUNTABLE
TO THE FATHER

*"My food is to do the will of Him who sent Me, and to finish
His work."*   —John 4:34 (NKJV)

In developing the spirit of accountability, we can have no better
example, once again, than Jesus Christ. Jesus referred continually
to His accountability to the Father, making statements such as
*"My food is to do the will of Him who sent Me, and to finish His
work"*(John 4:34 NKJV) and acknowledging the Father's affirmation of the Son's leadership: *"For the works that the Father has given
me to finish—the very works that I am doing—testify that the Father
has sent me"* (John 5:36). *"For on him [Jesus] God the Father has
placed his seal of approval"* (John 6:27).

The gospel of John gives us many additional examples of Jesus's
accountability to and relationship with the Father, including the
following: *"Jesus gave them this answer: 'Very truly I tell you, the Son
can do nothing by himself; he can do only what he sees his Father doing,
because whatever the Father does the Son also does'"* (John 5:19). *"By
myself I can do nothing; I judge only as I hear, and my judgment is just,
for I seek not to please myself but him who sent me"* (John 5:30). *"For
I have come down from heaven not to do my will but to do the will of
him who sent me"* (John 6:38).

To manifest the leadership spirit hidden within you, you must
embrace the attitude of accountability. Always be conscious that
you are responsible to those below you and above you for everything you say and do. Be cognizant that whatever you do as a leader
may be personal, but it is never totally private. Remember Paul's

words in his letter to the people of Philippi, in which he explained that Jesus was willingly accountable to the Father when He came to earth to serve and redeem us, and how we are to follow His pattern of accountability to God and to look out for the well-being of those around us: *"Let each of you look out not only for his own interests, but also for the interests of others. Let this mind be in you which was also in Christ Jesus, who, being in the form of God, did not consider it robbery to be equal with God, but made Himself of no reputation, taking the form of a bondservant, and coming in the likeness of men"* (Philippians 2:4–7 NKJV).

Your ultimate accountability is to the Creator of all leaders, who knows the thoughts and attitudes of your heart. The following are some additional guidelines for incorporating accountability into your life:

- Commit yourself to be accountable to your personal convictions.

- Establish the Word of God as your final judge and authority.

- Appoint and submit to a group of tested, respected, credible, and mature people for advice, correction, rebuke, and instruction.

- Choose friends who are committed to the high standards of the Word of God and give them the right to judge you by it.

Thought: Your ultimate accountability is to the Creator of all leaders, who knows the thoughts and attitudes of your heart.

Reading: John 8:28–29

— DAY 71 —
LEADERSHIP ATTITUDE #9: PERSISTENCE

*"Let us not become weary in doing good, for at the proper time
we will reap a harvest if we do not give up."* —Galatians 6:9

All true leaders also cultivate the ninth leadership attitude: the attitude of *persistence*. The spirit of leadership never gives up until it achieves its goal. It is a spirit that never quits.

Nothing in the world can take the place of persistence. Talent will not—nothing is more common than an unsuccessful person with talent. Genius will not—unrewarded genius is almost a proverb. Education will not—the world is filled with educated derelicts. Persistence and determination, however, are powerful forces.

Persistence is the product of faith that is generated by a purpose. It is:

+ The power to hold on, in spite of everything
+ The power to endure
+ The ability to face defeat again and again and not give up
+ The knack for pushing on in the face of difficulty, knowing that victory is yours
+ Taking pains to overcome every obstacle and to do what is necessary to reach your goals

Leaders persist because they have a firm grasp of their purposes, know where they are going, and are confident that they will arrive there. Their persistence is a manifestation that they hold a conviction about their futures based on the visions they have been given for their lives. True leaders believe that the attainment of their purposes is not optional but rather an obligation and a necessity, so they would never think of giving up.

Persistence, resilience, and perseverance are essential because opposition and setbacks are part of the process of fulfilling vision. Moreover, these qualities are especially needed when leaders experience failure. Passion for their purposes stirs them to get back up and keep moving toward their visions.

Remember, once a leader is inspired by a vision, a passion for accomplishing it comes alive within them. That passion motivates, energizes, renews, and fortifies a leader to be able to complete their generational assignment on earth. Passion feeds persistence, which enables them to push forward in the midst of obstacles, and it keeps them focused during times of seeming inactivity and lack of progress. A leader with passion is constantly fueled by their desire to complete their vision. Passion for purpose can be summed up by the words of Ecclesiastes 9:10: "*Whatever your hand finds to do, do it with all your might.*"

If you have stumbled in pursuing your purpose, start again, make new plans to take the place of old ones that aren't working, and stop only when you are finished!

⌣

Thought: Leaders persist because they have a firm grasp of their purposes, know where they are going, and are confident that they will arrive there.

Reading: Galatians 6:9–10

—Day 72—

THE PERSISTENCE OF THE WIDOW

"For everyone who asks receives; the one who seeks finds; and to the one who knocks, the door will be opened."

—Luke 11:10

Jesus understood the power of persistence, and He taught others about the importance of having this attitude. In fact, He told a wonderful parable, recorded in Luke's gospel, that gives us a perfect picture of persistence:

> *Suppose you have a friend, and you go to him at midnight and say, "Friend, lend me three loaves of bread; a friend of mine on a journey has come to me, and I have no food to offer him." And suppose the one inside answers, "Don't bother me. The door is already locked, and my children and I are in bed. I can't get up and give you anything." I tell you, even though he will not get up and give you the bread because of friendship, yet because of your shameless audacity he will surely get up and give you as much as you need. So I say to you: Ask and it will be given to you; seek and you will find; knock and the door will be opened to you. For everyone who asks receives; the one who seeks finds; and to the one who knocks, the door will be opened.* (Luke 11:5–10)

The above story illustrates the power that persistence can have in accomplishing what we truly desire. At another time, Jesus told a similar parable that encourages us that success comes to those who persist—not only in the natural realm, but also in the spiritual realm.

In a certain town there was a judge who neither feared God nor cared what people thought. And there was a widow in that town who kept coming to him with the plea, "Grant me justice against my adversary." For some time he refused. But finally he said to himself, "Even though I don't fear God or care what people think, yet because this widow keeps bothering me, I will see that she gets justice, so that she won't eventually come and attack me!" And the Lord said, "Listen to what the unjust judge says. And will not God bring about justice for his chosen ones, who cry out to him day and night? Will he keep putting them off? I tell you, he will see that they get justice, and quickly. However, when the Son of Man comes, will he find faith on the earth?"   (Luke 18:2–8)

As you develop the leadership spirit of persistence, keep in mind these truths about the nature of your Creator and His own persistence in carrying out His purposes for you: (1) God is faithful. (2) God does not lie. (3) God has established His Word. (4) Your purpose is already completed in Him. (5) God delights in you and considers you His child.

⌣

Thought: The spirit of leadership never gives up until it achieves its goal.

Reading: Matthew 7:7–8

— DAY 73 —

LEADERSHIP ATTITUDE #10: SELF-DISCIPLINE

"So I say, walk by the Spirit, and you will not gratify the desires of the flesh."   —Galatians 5:16

The tenth attitude of leadership is that of strong *self-discipline*. Any study of the characteristics of true leaders will reveal that they all exhibit self-discipline, usually motivated by a passion generated by a sense of purpose and vision. All leaders are "prisoners" of the passion of their purposes.

Genuine leaders understand that self-discipline is the manifestation of the highest form of government—self-government. The true spirit of leadership cultivates a self-control that regulates one's focus and orders one's life. The disciplined lifestyle distinguishes leaders from followers.

What is discipline? Discipline may be defined as self-imposed standards and restrictions stirred by a desire that is greater than the alternatives. It is self-policing. The nature of discipline is self-management regulated by a code of conduct in keeping with a set of goals and commitments dictated by an intended result. In other words, discipline is a series of decisions prescribed by a determined destiny.

The spirit of discipline is rooted in self-control, which is a fruit of the Spirit. As Paul taught the Galatian church, *"But the fruit of the Spirit is love, joy, peace, forbearance, kindness, goodness, faithfulness, gentleness and self-control. Against such things there is no law"* (Galatians 5:22–23).

Leaders live with an understanding of the following:

- He who cannot control his thoughts will never control himself.

- He who cannot rule himself will never control his life.

- He who cannot rule himself will never rule a nation.

- He who cannot control himself will be controlled by others.

Discipline leads to personal transformation. Leaders know that the most powerful kind of control is self-control because it is the hardest to master but reaps the greatest rewards. Therefore, they are more concerned with controlling themselves than with controlling other people.

According to *Merriam-Webster.com Dictionary*, the words *disciple* and *discipline* come from the same root word meaning "pupil."[17] A disciple is a student or learner who is dedicated to concentrated and focused instruction or is committed to learning to think like their teacher. This is why the followers of the ultimate teacher, Jesus Christ, were called His disciples, for it was His intent to take them through His "school of thought" and change their thinking so that they thought like Him.

A disciple is considered an understudy, one given to or submitted to the mentoring of a master teacher. They voluntarily surrender their will to the influence of the teacher in order to obtain the teacher's knowledge, thoughts, and philosophy for the purpose of personal transformation. Thus, as they practice self-control, all true leaders are students *of* life and *for* life.

Thought: The spirit of discipline is rooted in self-control, which is a fruit of the Spirit.

Reading: Galatians 5:16–26

---

17. *Merriam-Webster.com Dictionary*, s.v. "discipline," https://www.merriam-webster.com/dictionary/discipline.

— DAY 74 —

DISCIPLINE AND VISION

"Where there is no vision, the people are unrestrained."
—Proverbs 29:18 (NASB)

As we noted earlier, vision is the source of the leader's personal discipline. The man or woman with a clear vision lives a very focused life that requires strong self-discipline. This makes life very simple because your vision chooses the following:

+ Your use of time
+ Your priorities
+ Your friends
+ Your reading material
+ Your use of energy
+ Your hobbies
+ The movies you watch
+ Your diet
+ How you invest your money
+ Your to-do list
+ Your attitude toward life
+ Your life's plan
+ Your life.

Consider these questions: Are you self-disciplined? Do you impose high standards and strict parameters on yourself for the sake of fulfilling your purpose and vision? The following are some key characteristics of personal discipline.

Delayed gratification. Self-discipline means patiently waiting for the right and best results in life. Too many people want to rush the process—whether it is in regard to forming relationships, obtaining possessions, or achieving success—and they pursue an immediate "reward." A leader settles only for what is best in regard to their relationship with the Creator and their purpose and vision. They have learned when to reject immediate gratification for the sake of gaining greater benefits in the future.

Self-sacrifice. Leaders are willing to make sacrifices for the sake of service. They think more about those they are serving through their visions than about their own comfort. Entertainment and relaxation are not their principal goals in life. While they are aware that their bodies and minds need times of renewal and refreshing, they make the best use of their time that they can.

The pursuit of excellence. Leaders discipline themselves in the pursuit of excellence; they shun mediocrity. They strive to develop their skills and talents and to gain relevant knowledge and wisdom in order to accomplish their vision. While others allow laziness or apathy to set in, leaders discipline themselves to keep moving toward their goals by tapping into their original passions and accepting responsibility for completing tedious or difficult tasks. Leaders mold themselves to obtain what is best for their lives, and they will not settle for less than that.

To manifest the leadership spirit within you, you must cultivate self-discipline and regulate your thoughts and activities based on the results that you desire for your life. The spirit of leadership is a spirit of discipline.

Thought: Self-discipline means patiently waiting for the right and best results in life.

Reading: 1 Corinthians 10:13

— Day 75 —

LEADERSHIP ATTITUDE #11:
SELF-CULTIVATION

"Wisdom is the principal thing; therefore get wisdom. And in all your getting, get understanding." —Proverbs 4:7 (NKJV)

True leaders possess the leadership attitude of *self-cultivation,* a passion for personal development. Some marks of a genuine spirit of leadership are a desire and commitment to gain knowledge and insights, to keep improving oneself, and to learn from others.

Leaders are always looking for opportunities to advance their knowledge. They create their own learning opportunities and facilitate their own educational environments. Their personal collection of books is often their greatest possession. Leaders understand that they must never stop expanding their knowledge base, even extending their knowledge beyond their particular areas of focus in order to be versatile when necessary.

Great leaders love knowledge, but they don't just take it in. They *live* the principles they have learned until these principles become a part of their lives. We are not just to absorb knowledge for its own sake. It is the purposeful *application* of knowledge and the principles we derive from that knowledge that will enable us to lead effectively.

In addition, we must not only gain and apply knowledge, but we must also combine it with wisdom. Some people have advanced academic degrees but still can't seem to get along with others on the job. They have knowledge but lack wisdom regarding how to relate to their coworkers. Wisdom should not be confused with education.

Proverbs 4:7 says, *"Wisdom is the principal thing; therefore get wisdom. And in all your getting, get understanding"* (NKJV). Wisdom is the ability to use knowledge effectively. It is having a clear understanding of how various parts and principles relate to one another. It means having a clear perspective. Wisdom protects us from abusing knowledge by enabling us to apply it properly and effectively. It enables us to put our knowledge into a context that helps both us and others.

Again, wisdom is the ability to use knowledge *effectively*. Many people have knowledge, but not all have wisdom or common sense. Many people have information, but they have no revelation. The Scriptures teach that wisdom comes *"from above"* (James 3:17 NKJV, KJV). The source of true wisdom is God.

> *My son, if you accept my words and store up my commands within you, turning your ear to wisdom and applying your heart to understanding—indeed, if you call out for insight and cry aloud for understanding, and if you look for it as for silver and search for it as for hidden treasure, then you will understand the fear of the LORD and find the knowledge of God. For the LORD gives wisdom, and from his mouth come knowledge and understanding.* (Proverbs 2:1–6)

> *Instruct the wise and they will be wiser still; teach the righteous and they will add to their learning. The fear of the Lord is the beginning of wisdom, and knowledge of the Holy One is understanding.* (Proverbs 9:9–10)

Thought: A leader must have a dynamic relationship with the Source of wisdom and use the wisdom they receive in living out their life.

Reading: Proverbs 1:1–5

LEADERSHIP ATTITUDE #12: MENTORSHIP OF YOUR SUCCESSORS

"To Timothy my true son in the faith: Grace, mercy and peace from God the Father and Christ Jesus our Lord."
—1 Timothy 1:2

The twelfth attitude that is essential for the spirit of leadership is the attitude of *mentorship of your successors*, which we might also call "legacy." It is my conviction that the ultimate purpose of the spirit of leadership in any endeavor—whether it is business, religion, politics, sports, medicine, education, or another area—is not the accomplishment of goals or the achievement of quotas but rather the leader's legacy through their successors. True leadership is concerned more about people than products, more about mankind than money. It is measured by the people you "produce." Otherwise, after you pass on from this generation, your vision could die with you.

Therefore, the greatest investment in leadership is not in things but in people. Even though we are necessarily involved in a variety of activities to fulfill our visions, we must ask, "In whom am I investing to produce better leaders in the future and after my generation?" Let me reemphasize that the most valuable investment anyone can make is in another person, not in a piece of property or equipment. People who intend to extend their lives through projects will ultimately fail.

Jesus Christ never built a building, and He never produced a product. He created *people* who could do and lead as He did. Remember that *"we are God's handiwork, created in Christ Jesus* to do good works, which God prepared in advance for us to do" (Ephesians 2:10). Jesus changed the course of history, and the leaders He trained were said to have "turned the world upside down" (Acts 17:6 NKJV, KJV).

The greatest expression of this leadership principle of succession is found in this statement of Jesus to the leaders that He developed: "All authority in heaven and on earth has been given to me. Therefore go and make disciples [students] of all nations" (Matthew 28:18–19). With these words, Jesus defined the purpose of authority, which is to transfer and release the authority of others. He obviously did not see authority as permission to lord it over others or to wield power in the affairs of men. Rather, He saw it as a vehicle to allow others the freedom to develop and reach their full potential.

Mentoring is a nonnegotiable function of successful leadership. A genuine leader knows that their most significant contribution to the future is their successor or successors.

Since creating leaders is the ultimate purpose of leadership, I hope you will be stirred to refocus your interests regarding your priority in leadership. No matter how great your vision, it is important to produce visionaries to carry it on. You must always remember this: your goal is not to *amass followers* but to *train leaders*.

⌒

Thoughts: The greatest investment in leadership is not in things but in people.

Reading: 1 Timothy 1:1–5

— DAY 77 —

JESUS'S TRANSFER OF LEADERSHIP

"Very truly I tell you, whoever believes in me will do the works I have been doing, and they will do even greater things than these, because I am going to the Father."   —John 14:12

As a leader, you should measure your success and effectiveness by the diminishing degree of your followers' dependency on you. The less they need you, the more effective you are. This principle is seen throughout Scripture as it continually manifests itself in God's encounters with humanity.

Jesus expressed His anticipation of the transition from follower to leader on many occasions. He told His disciples, *"Very truly I tell you, whoever believes in me will do the works I have been doing, and they will do even greater things than these, because I am going to the Father. And I will do whatever you ask in my name, so that the Father may be glorified in the Son"* (John 14:12–13). These words indicate that Jesus's purpose for training His disciples was to teach them how to be responsible, effective leaders.

If we do not fulfill our purpose of training leaders, then those who come after us cannot do "greater things." In addition, this verse reveals that Jesus Christ was not attached to His position on earth, and that He saw the transfer of that position to His disciples—His leaders-in-training—as progress. Jesus was indicating that His remaining on earth would hinder the leadership progress of these disciples.

Jesus clearly stated His philosophy of the purpose of leadership when He said, *"But very truly I tell you, it is for your good that I am going away. Unless I go away, the Advocate [God's Spirit] will not* come to you; but if I go, I will send him to you" (John 16:7). Did He really say it was for their *good* that He was going away? This seems like a very strange thing for a leader to state. The average leader thinks in the opposite way: "I don't want to leave this position. I'm not going to let anyone take it from me." The ultimate proof of Jesus's success as a leader was the fact that He *left.* He saw effective leadership as the ability to release the potential of others and to inspire them to fulfill that potential.

Additionally, the assignment Jesus gave to the leadership of the church, as presented in Paul's letter to the Ephesians, clearly signifies the purpose of leadership:

> So Christ himself gave the apostles, the prophets, the evangelists, the pastors and teachers, to equip [train] his people for works of service, so that the body of Christ may be built up until we all reach unity in the faith and in the knowledge of the Son of God and become mature, attaining to the whole measure of the fullness of Christ.　　(Ephesians 4:11–13)

Thought: The purpose of leadership is to produce a more effective generation of leaders after us by identifying, developing, and refining the hidden leader in every follower.

Reading: John 20:19–22

—DAY 78—

DON'T GIVE UP—GIVE OVER!

"The LORD said to Joshua son of Nun, Moses' aide: '...As I was with Moses, so I will be with you.'" —Joshua 1:1, 5

Most leaders have become so attached to their positions that they have allowed these positions to become synonymous with their worth and value. True leaders who understand their design in creation do not confuse their value with their professions or their self-esteem with their assignments. They are always aware that assignments are dispensable but worth is permanent because it comes from God. This is why they don't mind giving over an assignment to someone else. They know they don't lose their worth or their purpose when they give a particular responsibility to others.

A lack of leadership transfer is a problem that can be found in all realms of life—political, religious, civic, business, and family. One of the main reasons for this is that people feel as if they are "giving up" their leadership when they transfer authority to others. What we need to realize is that we do not give *up* our leadership. We give it *over*. If you give it up, it's as if you have *lost* something. Giving it over means you have *continued* something.

Several good examples from the Scriptures of those who gave over their leadership are Moses, whose successor was Joshua; Paul, whose successor and *"true son in the faith"* (1 Timothy 1:2) was Timothy; and, of course, Jesus Christ, who entrusted the leadership of His brand-new church to Peter and the other disciples after He returned to God the Father in heaven.

Joshua had served as Moses's right-hand man for forty years. When it came time for Moses to die and Joshua to lead the Israelites into the promised land, *"the LORD said to Moses, 'Now the day of your death is near. Call Joshua and present yourselves at the tent of meeting, where I will commission him.' So Moses and Joshua came and presented themselves at the tent of meeting"* (Deuteronomy 31:14). Moses was still alive when Joshua was commissioned as his successor and placed in the position of authority before all the Israelites. Everyone knew that Joshua was now in charge. After Moses's death, *"The LORD said to Joshua son of Nun, Moses' aide: '...As I was with Moses, so I will be with you'"* (Joshua 1:1, 5).

Paul expressed the leadership principle of transferring and releasing authority to others when he told Timothy, *"And the things you have heard me say in the presence of many witnesses entrust to reliable people who will also be qualified to teach others"* (2 Timothy 2:2).

Jesus passed authority to Peter when He told him, *"Feed my lambs"* (John 21:15), *"Take care of my sheep"* (verse 16), and *"Feed my sheep"* (verse 17). And after Jesus transferred authority, the whole organization grew under Peter once he had received the Holy Spirit, of whom Jesus had said, *"The Advocate, the Holy Spirit, whom the Father will send in my name, will teach you all things and will remind you of everything I have said to you"* (John 14:26).

⌒

Thought: A leader mentors his successors by providing vision, inspiration, and guidance, producing leaders who can carry on the purpose.

Reading: 1 Kings 19:15–21

TRUE LEADERS COMMIT TO VALUES

*"And whatever you do, whether in word or deed, do it all in
the name of the Lord Jesus, giving thanks to God the Father
through him."*   —Colossians 3:17

Leaders commit to spiritual and moral truths that form their character and help them to carry out their unique purpose and vision. Values are natural components in the successful realization of a leader's vision. True leadership always includes a personal code of ethics and standards that safeguard the character necessary for the leader to pursue and fulfill their purpose. It is vital for a leader to develop their own sense of self and their role in the world. It is equally vital for a leader to test themselves and their beliefs and principles. The world longs for people who will stand up for what they believe, even if they must stand alone, because we can have confidence in such people to have courage and integrity as they lead.

A leader must have an integration of values. You can't have humility without courage, you can't have courage without compassion, and you can't have compassion without steadiness if you want to be an effective leader.

Leadership is ultimately measured by what it values. True leadership should value human life, human dignity, human equality, human rights, and human security. To become a leader, you must commit to principles and values for the development of your character and the fulfillment of your God-given destiny.

In addition, leadership requires the willingness to sacrifice pleasure for the protection of purpose. It necessitates a dedication to principles more than to profit and popularity; it places convictions above convenience; it is more concerned with excellence than with expediency. And, as we noted earlier, true leaders are always sensitive to spiritual accountability and aware of their obligation to divine authority.

Thus, leadership involves the total person and cannot be relegated only to a "professional compartment" of our lives. Many people insist that their personal lives should not be linked with their professional positions as leaders, and that their activities and behaviors outside their leadership roles have no bearing on their ability to perform. This grave error has accounted for the tragic downfall of many great men and women who attempted to violate this principle of the integration of the complete self in leadership.

No matter what realm of life we may discuss, principles and values are all-important with regard to quality of life—for both the leader and those whom they influence and affect. True leadership cannot be separated from the basic values that produce good, sound character.

⌣

Thought: Leaders commit to spiritual and moral truths that form their character and help them to carry out a unique purpose and vision.

Reading: Colossians 3:12–14

— DAY 80 —

LEAD ACCORDING TO GOD'S SPIRIT

"I pray that out of his glorious riches he may strengthen you with power through his Spirit in your inner being."
—Ephesians 3:16

Do you seek to lead according to your abilities alone, or do you look to the Holy Spirit for wisdom and strength? We were created to operate by the Spirit of God. Therefore, if any other spirit influences our lives, we are unable to become or function as the leaders we were designed to be. Just as an automobile was created to operate on gasoline, if a person is not filled with this necessary source of "energy," they are unable to truly perform their God-given purpose. If a car's tank is filled with glue instead of gasoline, the vehicle will malfunction, and its vital components will eventually be destroyed. Likewise, if a person does not have a vital connection with God and is not filled with His Spirit, that individual will malfunction. We learn to discern our life's purpose and vision through our relationship with the Creator and by a continual intake of His Word, because genuine vision is always in alignment with His nature and character and revealed by His Spirit.

Every true leader should have a strong spiritual commitment to follow the leading of God's Spirit. If you desire to become an effective leader, you must strengthen your relationship with your Creator and continue to mature in your spiritual life. Spiritual maturity naturally incorporates many of the values you need to be a leader.

The leader is responsible for securing the trust, confidence, and commitment of their followers by adhering to moral, ethical, and spiritual principles. It is essential that the true leader be led by the Spirit and be vigilant in guarding their spirit, mind, and body from any compromise that would render them untrustworthy and unrespectable in the sight of others. They need to adhere to the highest principles of honor, integrity, morality, and self-respect. They must commit to spiritual and ethical values and principles to successfully fulfill their call to genuine leadership.

The apostle Paul outlined for his leader-in-training, Timothy, many of the values that are needed for true leadership. In every field of leadership, these values are essential requirements:

> Now the overseer is to be above reproach, faithful to his wife, temperate, self-controlled, respectable, hospitable, able to teach, not given to drunkenness, not violent but gentle, not quarrelsome, not a lover of money. He must manage his own family well and see that his children obey him, and he must do so in a manner worthy of full respect. (If anyone does not know how to manage his own family, how can he take care of God's church?) He must not be a recent convert, or he may become conceited and fall under the same judgment as the devil. He must also have a good reputation with outsiders, so that he will not fall into disgrace and into the devil's trap.
>
> (1 Timothy 3:2–7)

Thought: We were created to operate by the Spirit of God.

Reading: Ephesians 3:14–19

THE VALUES OF FAITHFULNESS AND INTEGRITY

"And the things that you have heard from me among many witnesses, commit these to faithful men who will be able to teach others also." —2 Timothy 2:2 (NKJV)

Genuine leaders are individuals whose character has been tested, proven, and established as being faithful and trustworthy. *Faithfulness* is a virtue of character that applies to all aspects of leadership. Each of us has been given gifts and talents, but we must be faithful to use them. You might have potential as a piano player, but if you don't make time to practice, your talent will not serve you well. Similarly, being a talented leader isn't enough; you must also be faithful to develop the inner character of leadership.

It's easier to get excited about a vision than it is to remain faithful to it. Many people are well-meaning and desire to serve as leaders, but it is those who are faithful to what they have already been given who are ushered into leadership. God's Word tells us that faithfulness in the little things is the qualification for promotion to bigger things: *"He who is faithful in what is least is faithful also in much.... Therefore if you have not been faithful in the unrighteous mammon, who will commit to your trust the true riches? And if you have not been faithful in what is another man's, who will give you what is your own?"* (Luke 16:10–12 NKJV).

Faithfulness in caring for and using what we have been given is a quality of maturity. I have found that one proof of a man or woman's faithfulness in leadership is their commitment to their spouse. We call people who break their marriage vows "unfaithful." An important aspect of faithfulness is that your word can be trusted. If your word cannot be trusted in the marriage relationship, then it cannot be trusted in other areas of life.

Personal *integrity* is another value of leaders. Leaders in all walks of life must demonstrate their commitment to the highest ideals and principles of God's Word, never compromising the standards of truth and integrity. There is a whole range of circumstances in which integrity is needed in a leader. The more familiar you are with God's Word, the more you will be able to recognize pitfalls to your integrity and seek to maintain values consistent with the nature of the Creator.

Leadership author Warren Bennis wrote, "Integrity is the basis of trust.... It is the one quality that cannot be acquired but must be earned. It is given by co-workers and followers, and without it, the leader can't function."[18]

When we consider leaders in history, George Washington is an excellent example of integrity. Washington served alongside the most intelligent, gifted, and influential men of the remarkable group of leaders who came together during the American Revolution—men such as Benjamin Franklin, John Adams, Thomas Jefferson, and Alexander Hamilton. Yet all of them considered Washington to be the greatest man they knew. Why? His personal integrity caused these powerful and talented men to respect and admire him as their undisputed leader.

Thought: Leaders in all walks of life must demonstrate their commitment to the highest ideals and principles of the Word of God.

Reading: 2 Timothy 2:1–7

---

18. Warren G. Bennis, *On Becoming a Leader* (New York: Basic Books, 2003), 33.

— Day 82 —

THE VALUES OF STEADINESS AND SELF-CONTROL

"Therefore, my beloved brethren, be steadfast, immovable, always abounding in the work of the Lord, knowing that your labor is not in vain in the Lord."
—1 Corinthians 15:58 (NKJV)

Embracing the value of *steadiness* is vital for a leader. How do you react when people say something unexpected or when situations don't go as you would like? Are you able to respond in a constructive way? When a problem or crisis occurs, are you able to think through your options calmly and positively? Can you maintain the confidence of those looking to you for leadership? This kind of steadiness is a much-needed trait among leaders today. The book of Proverbs warns us, *"Do you see someone who speaks in haste? There is more hope for a fool than for them.... An angry person stirs up conflict, and a hot-tempered person commits many sins"* (Proverbs 29:20, 22).

James, a leader in the first-century church, encouraged the recipients of his teachings, *"Everyone should be quick to listen, slow to speak and slow to become angry"* (James 1:19). If you are steadfast, it means you respond with calmness and gentleness the first time, the second time, and the ninetieth time. You don't interrupt people, assume you know what they are going to say, or fly off the handle. You value the worth and dignity of those around you.

The value of *self-control*, particularly as it relates to standing against temptation, is another essential value. *"Like a city whose walls are broken through is a person who lacks self-control"* (Proverbs

25:28). Whenever you are placed in a position of leadership, you automatically become a target of temptation. If a thousand people are gathered together, and one person is put above the crowd, that person becomes an easier target than if they were still part of the crowd. In other words, when you become a leader, you are usually in a highly visible position, and you become attractive to many interests.

While external temptations will inevitably come, leaders must call upon their inner strength and commitment to withstand them. That strength includes the encouragement and power of God's Spirit, who lives within them. *"No temptation has overtaken you except what is common to mankind. And God is faithful; he will not let you be tempted beyond what you can bear. But when you are tempted, he will also provide a way out so that you can endure it"* (1 Corinthians 10:13).

Inner strength also refers to a leader's fortitude, which they have established ahead of time by setting moral standards that they are committed to maintaining, regardless of the circumstances.

If you desire to be a leader, look for temptation's traps. They are all around you. *"Be alert and of sober mind. Your enemy the devil prowls around like a roaring lion looking for someone to devour. Resist him, standing firm in the faith"* (1 Peter 5:8–9).

⌒

Thought: Whenever you are placed in a position of leadership, you automatically become a target of temptation.

Reading: James 1:19–27

— DAY 83 —

THE VALUE OF TRUSTWORTHINESS

"The works of his hands are faithful and just; all his precepts are trustworthy."   —Psalm 111:7

If the source of leadership is inspiration, and the life of leadership is confidence, then the fuel of leadership is trust. That is why the value of *trustworthiness* is so indispensable. To become an effective leader, you must earn the trust of others. We have seen that effective leadership is essentially built on the foundation of inspirational power and an honorable life that produces confidence in one's character. Thus, trustworthiness is a product of time and integrity. It is produced by character and competence—who you are and what you do.

God is trustworthy toward us, and we can reflect His nature to others as we learn from Him. *"The works of his hands are faithful and just; all his precepts are trustworthy. They are established for ever and ever, enacted in faithfulness and uprightness"* (Psalm 111:7–8).

Trustworthy leaders are sought out for advice and assistance in sensitive situations. Daniel is an example of such a leader. When we think of Daniel, we often think of his being thrown into the lions' den and of the miracle from God that saved him from death. (See Daniel 6:1–23.) But that incident was only a few hours of Daniel's life, which was full of many other events. Daniel 6:1–2 reads, *"It pleased Darius* [the king] *to appoint 120 satraps to rule throughout the kingdom, with three administrators over them, one of whom was Daniel."* This man of God was a Spirit-filled, trustworthy government official. God wants us where the action is, and Daniel was right there.

Daniel 6:4 says, *"They could find no corruption in him, because he was trustworthy and neither corrupt nor negligent."* Wouldn't it be wonderful to work with someone who wasn't negligent, someone who kept their word? Again, trust is not a gift or a talent but a product of time-tested character forged in the midst of life's trials. A time-tested life is the raw material of character and trust.

If you want to become the leader you have the potential to be, remember that it is vital to test yourself and your beliefs and principles so that you will become a trustworthy person. You must earn the trust of others by cultivating and maintaining personal character through a steadfast commitment to strong values. Leaders develop the characteristics that qualify them for a distinguished place of trustworthiness.

If we want effective, just, and qualified leaders in our world today, we must become men and women who are filled with God's Spirit and led by His Word for the purpose of serving others. Continue to develop your spiritual life by strengthening your relationship with God, the Supreme Leader, through Jesus Christ, and learning His nature and ways. Be willing to step forward and offer your service in an honorable way to the community and nation in which you live through your gifts and spheres of influence.

⌒

Thought: Trustworthiness is a product of character and competence—who you are and what you do.

Reading: Psalm 111:1–8

— DAY 84 —

THE VALUE OF COURAGE

"Fear of man will prove to be a snare, but whoever trusts in the Lord is kept safe." —Proverbs 29:25

The next value we must hold to is *courage*. God cannot use someone in a leadership position who is afraid of other people. Leaders who have confidence in God and their own abilities have no fear of men. The prophet Isaiah recorded this admonishment from God to His people: *"I, even I, am he who comforts you. Who are you that you fear mere mortals, human beings who are but grass?"* (Isaiah 51:12).

Consider these questions: How do you behave when you're with your boss? Do you say what you need to? Or do you say what you think they want to hear? If you have to talk to your boss about something that's on your mind, do you think about it for twelve months, go to the door of their office, and then say to yourself, "Let me think about this some more"? Or do you go right in with an attitude of respect and speak your mind? Of course, wisdom and discretion are needed in such circumstances. However, some people never act in a courageous way because they already believe they're going to be turned down or that failure is inevitable.

The Bible says, *"Fear of man will prove to be a snare"* (Proverbs 29:25). A snare is the same thing as a trap. When you're caught in a trap, you can't move. You can't express what you want to, and so you never progress in your leadership. Perhaps you haven't been promoted because your boss sees you as a person who has no confidence in yourself. True leaders love confident people.

Robert Coles, noted author and psychiatrist, said this of Abraham Lincoln:

> Lincoln did not go to Gettysburg having commissioned a poll to find out what would sell in Gettysburg. There were no people with percentages for him, cautioning him about this group or that group or what they found in exit polls a year earlier. When will we have the courage of Lincoln?[19]

To have courage also means to stand up on your strength. For years and years, I used to pray for strength. Guess what? I never got an ounce. Why? Because we already have all the strength we need. Do you know where your strength comes from? Joy. *"The joy of the* LORD *is your strength"* (Nehemiah 8:10). You can't pray for strength before you find your joy. What happens in this world is not supposed to affect your joy, for true joy comes from within. Joy in the Lord is the secret of our strength. Remember these words of encouragement from God: *"Fear not, for I am with you; be not dismayed, for I am your God. I will strengthen you, yes, I will help you, I will uphold you with My righteous right hand"* (Isaiah 41:10 NKJV).

Change your course. Be courageous.

Thought: People who have confidence in God and their own abilities have no fear of men.

Reading: Isaiah 41:8–10

19. Robert Coles, "Quotes," Goodreads, https://www.goodreads.com/quotes/32263-abraham-lincoln-did-not-go-to-gettysburg-having-commissioned-a.

THE VALUE OF HUMILITY

"Do nothing out of selfish ambition or vain conceit. Rather, in humility value others above yourselves." —Philippians 2:3

What is humility? Humility is the ability to be yourself. The word *humble* comes from the Latin root word *humus*, meaning "earth." *Humility* denotes earthiness or an awareness of one's true essence. (See Genesis 2:7.) Being humble, therefore, does not mean degrading or reducing oneself in the estimation of another, but rather having a consciousness, acceptance, and appreciation of one's true worth and value. In this regard, you cannot "decide" to be humble because it is not something you decide to be; it is what you are. Leaders are individuals who have discovered their true selves and know who they are. Thus, *true leaders are naturally humble*, in the full sense of the word.

Humility is not foolishness. It doesn't mean that you allow yourself to be pressured to do something because someone puts you on a guilt trip. Humility is the ability to control knowledge and power, even though you know they are yours to exercise. It is speaking your knowledge at the right time, in the right words, and to the right person.

Paul wrote to his protégé, Timothy, that a leader should not be a new convert and inexperienced because they might be tempted to become conceited from being placed in a position over others. (See 1 Timothy 3:6.) A person inexperienced in the values and principles of leadership could easily miss the whole point of leadership and use it for selfish ambition, personal gain, and a false sense of security. But one who has worked hard to understand leadership and become an honorable and mature leader will exhibit the quality of humility.

Humility is a trait that results from our acknowledgment of God's love and mercy in our lives. Jesus exemplified humility at the Last Supper when He met with the disciples to celebrate the Passover meal. It was a custom in those days that before a meal was served, a servant washed the feet of the arriving guests. There were no servants when Jesus and the disciples arrived for dinner, but their feet needed to be washed just the same.

I can just see the disciples arguing among themselves about who would do this menial task. As they were arguing, Jesus took a towel and a washbasin and began to do the job Himself. The disciples were stunned into silence. Jesus had gotten their attention, and they learned a valuable lesson on the true meaning of leadership. He told them:

> *Now that I, your Lord and Teacher, have washed your feet, you also should wash one another's feet. I have set you an example that you should do as I have done for you. Very truly I tell you, no servant is greater than his master, nor is a messenger greater than the one who sent him. Now that you know these things, you will be blessed if you do them.*
>
> (John 13:14–17)

Thought: Humility is knowing who you are and accepting it without boasting.

Readings: Proverbs 11:2; 22:4

—DAY 86—

THE VALUES OF FORGIVENESS
AND GRATITUDE

"And forgive us our debts, as we also have forgiven our debtors."
                                                    —Matthew 6:12

T rue leaders are so secure in their relationship with God that they can forgive and ask for forgiveness without hesitation. "[Love] *keeps no record of wrongs*" (1 Corinthians 13:5). Leaders reject petty, childish resentments. They can't afford to overreact to negative behaviors, criticism, or human weakness. They don't waste time on such things. They know that God desires for us to forgive even major offenses, just as He has forgiven us. When Peter wanted to know how many times we should forgive others, Jesus replied, *"I tell you, not seven times, but seventy-seven times"* (Matthew 18:22). Jesus prayed for those who crucified Him, *"Father, forgive them, for they do not know what they are doing"* (Luke 23:34). Stephen, one of the leaders of the first-century church, was stoned to death. And as he was dying, he prayed, *"Lord, do not hold this sin against them"* (Acts 7:60).

True leaders forgive and don't carry grudges. A person may be hurt by someone, and ten years later, when they see that individual again, they still want to get even. If you harbor unforgiveness, you negate the possibility of being used effectively by God.

True leaders also do not feel superior when they discover the weaknesses of others. They are aware that they, too, have weaknesses. They realize that behavior and potential are two different things, and they believe in the inherent potential of all people. They believe in the ability of others to change. They feel grateful for their blessings and are able to naturally and compassionately forgive the offenses of others. True leaders know that their feelings are not the same things as facts, and they act on that awareness. This requires strong control over their thoughts, and it also fosters humility within them.

Additionally, a true leader lives in a constant state of gratitude to the Creator for His love and provision and for the opportunity to pursue their purpose and vision. *"Give thanks to the LORD, for he is good; his love endures forever"* (Psalm 107:1). Paul was a man filled with thanksgiving and gratitude. At various times, he wrote about the importance of giving thanks to a loving, faithful God.

> *Always giving thanks to God the Father for everything, in the name of our Lord Jesus Christ.* (Ephesians 5:20)

> *And whatever you do, whether in word or deed, do it all in the name of the Lord Jesus, giving thanks to God the Father through him.* (Colossians 3:17)

> *Devote yourselves to prayer, keeping alert in it with an attitude of thanksgiving.* (Colossians 4:2 NASB)

> *Giving thanks in all circumstances, for this is God's will for you in Christ Jesus.* (1 Thessalonians 5:18)

What are you thankful and grateful for today? Is there anyone you need to forgive?

⌒

Thought: Having a grateful attitude toward God and others will give you strength and peace and will set a positive tone for your leadership.

Reading: Matthew 6:9–14

— DAY 87 —

THE VALUE OF EMPOWERING OTHERS

"Let us therefore make every effort to do what leads to peace and to mutual edification."   —Romans 14:19

Leadership never exists for itself. It exists for the purpose of guiding others to a better future, enabling them to develop in greater ways, helping them to improve themselves, and inspiring them to believe that anything is possible. Leadership sets standards for people and influences them positively, giving them hope and deep conviction about their own abilities to achieve greatness. Leadership *empowers*.

Leadership considers success a corporate issue and is therefore lavish in its appreciation of everyone. It never takes credit; it always distributes credit. It knows what people need—empathy, respect, love, recognition, appreciation, encouragement, integrity, trust, and faith—and is dedicated to meeting these needs. Leadership builds people to build a vision to build a future.

True leadership is, therefore, a commitment to people. Leadership invests time, resources, energy, and experience in the empowerment of others. Remember, a leader's vision cannot be accomplished with an individualist attitude. No great work was ever done by just one person. The basic function of the leader (after inspiring others in their vision) is to provide an environment that fosters mutual respect and builds a complementary, cohesive team where each unique strength is made productive and each weakness is made irrelevant.

To empower others, leaders set an example. A leader recognizes that the tone and standards they set for the accomplishment of their vision have a direct bearing on their ability to empower others. If they influence, in a positive way, those who share their vision, progress will be made. If they resort to authoritarian power, unjust practices, or carelessness, they jeopardize the vision. The quality and integrity of daily advancement toward the vision are the leader's responsibility. Leaders must act with integrity toward others, modeling what is expected and clarifying the necessary requirements of the vision.

Leaders empower followers by recognizing the value of taking responsibility and encouraging that quality in themselves and others. King Solomon wrote, *"I have seen the burden God has laid on the human race"* (Ecclesiastes 3:10). The word *"burden"* in the Hebrew could actually be translated as "a heavy responsibility," "occupation," or "task." It could also be described as a "responsible urge." Every human being comes to earth with a purpose or responsibility that, in a sense, weighs on them throughout their life. They have a continual need or urge to fulfill it.

Because of God's unique purpose for each of us, He has placed a "responsible urge" in our hearts. Solomon also wrote, *"He has also set eternity* [a sense of divine purpose] *in the human heart"* (Ecclesiastes 3:11). Consider that God has empowered you to be a leader in your generation. He has put into your heart a purpose and a vision that can translate the unseen into the seen. Imagine— His eternal purposes intersect with time and the physical world in *your* life and heart! The very essence of life is for you to find God's purpose and fulfill it, empowering others as you do. Will you respond to His call from eternity?

⌒

Thought: True leadership is a commitment to people.

Reading: Ecclesiastes 3:10–11

— DAY 88 —

EVALUATE YOURSELF BY YOUR PURPOSE

"You did not choose me, but I chose you and appointed you so that you might go and bear fruit—fruit that will last."
—John 15:16

Every person, from their own perspective, desires to be successful. What is true success? Success can be defined as the efficient and effective completion of an assigned task to the level of expectation of the one who gave the assignment. In other words, *true success is the fulfillment of the original purpose.* Success is not measured by what you have done compared to what others have done, but rather by what you have done compared to what you were called to do. Consequently, the true essence of effectiveness is the successful completion of the correct assignment or purpose. In this sense, effectiveness is not doing things right but doing the right thing.

Leaders who are secure in their sense of self-worth do not evaluate themselves in light of others. It is natural to measure the success of leadership by the accomplishment of objectives. However, we can be tempted to measure our success by a *comparison* to the accomplishments of others. Doing so can lead to the development of a jealous spirit. *True leaders do not measure their success by comparing themselves to others but by evaluating how they are fulfilling their own purpose and vision.*

If you are sure of your assignment in life, then you are free from competition and comparison, and thus jealousy. Guard your heart and mind against a destructive spirit of deceit and envy. There is no need for it. You are the only one who can do what you were born to do. God will not reward you for competition but for obedience to Him and to the vision He has entrusted to you.

The Bible says that God sought you out, not the other way around. (See John 15:16.) He has a plan for your life, and you do not need to feel inferior to anyone else. To become a leader, you must possess a deep sense of security, which represents your recognition of your identity in God, your awareness of your self-worth, your emotional anchoring, and your personal strength.

Leaders are never intimidated by anyone because they have self-confidence that is grounded in Christ. They are aware that nobody is better or worse than they are, just different. They know that all people have the same value before God.

A true leader understands that any measure of popularity they have is simply a temporary reaction of people to their gifts and position and does not reflect who they are as a person. They are more concerned about pleasing God than about being popular with people. They have "an audience of One," as some have called it. They do not confuse applause with affirmation. They do not confuse temporary awards with eternal reward.

Thought: True leaders do not measure their success by comparing themselves to others but by evaluating how they are fulfilling their own purpose and vision.

Reading: John 15:9–16

"THE LEADER'S 'BE-ATTITUDES'"

"[You] have put on the new self, which is being renewed in knowledge in the image of its Creator." —Colossians 3:10

It is my wholehearted belief that true leadership is 20 percent talent, skill, and technical knowledge and 80 percent attitude. Together, we have learned that our attitude can be transformed when we discover our true value and purpose, established by God at creation: we were made in God's image, and we have been given an inherent *leadership spirit*. Experiencing a transformation in our attitude and mindset will ignite our *spirit of leadership* and activate our potential and our commitment to achieve. The leadership attitude is more concerned with fully expressing itself than with attempting to prove itself to others.

In addition to the twelve powerful attitudes and ten values for leadership presented earlier, true leadership requires a number of other attributes that are indispensable for the effective fulfillment of vision in the twenty-first century. The following are what I call "Leadership Attitudes-to-Be," or "The Leader's 'Be-Attitudes,'" some of which we have touched on in previous devotions but are important to review so we can establish them in our lives. They describe the mindset that every leader must embrace, cultivate, and exhibit in their exercise of leadership.

THE LEADER'S BE-ATTITUDES

1. *The spirit of resilience:* the ability to see failure as temporary and a necessary step to success

2. *The spirit of patience*: a belief in the potential of change and the ability to wait for it

3. *The spirit of compassion*: a sensitivity to the worth of others

4. *The spirit of self-value*: a belief in one's importance to the world

5. *The spirit of self-confidence*: a trust in one's inherent abilities

6. *The spirit of perseverance*: the ability never to give up or surrender to the context of a situation

7. *The spirit of strategic thinking*: the ability to plan rather than panic

8. *The spirit of time management*: the conscious application of time to goals

9. *The spirit of high tolerance for diversity*: a belief in the beauty and strength of variety

As we have discussed throughout this devotional, *attitude* is the key to the manifestation of your true leadership potential. What leadership attitudes are you seeking to develop today?

Thought: It is my wholehearted belief that true leadership is 20 percent talent, skill, and technical knowledge and 80 percent attitude.

Reading: Colossians 3:10–14

—Day 90—

LEADERSHIP: OUR PAST AND OUR DESTINY

"In him we were also chosen, having been predestined according to the plan of him who works out everything in conformity with the purpose of his will." —Ephesians 1:11

Leadership is both an art and a science: it is innate and yet learned; it is inherent and yet must be developed. True leadership is the hope of the future of our world and will determine the success or failure of our homes, communities, cities, and nations. If we are going to discover the true leadership potential that resides within us, we will have to consult and refer to our omnipotent Creator for the revelation of our leadership capacity and reconnect to the essence of our leadership assignment.

Leadership is both our past and our destiny. It is the only thing that will fulfill our natural passion for greatness. You were born to lead—settle for nothing less. Your generation and your world await your manifestation. Do it for the unborn generations who are meant to build on the foundation of your success as a leader. Remember, the difference between a follower and a leader is attitude. We must possess the attitude of leadership. As I wrote earlier, we must think, talk, walk, dress, act, respond, decide, plan, work, relate, and live like leaders. You have the leadership spirit; now you need the attitude of leadership.

I challenge you to spend time with the Creator and discover the awesome joy it is to receive the power and spirit of dominion available through an intimate relationship with Him. I encourage you to submit to Jesus Christ—the Authorized Dealer whom the

Father sent to reconnect you to yourself and to His purpose and plan for your life.

Cultivate the same attitude that eighty-five-year-old Caleb had when following Joshua into the promised land. Forty-five years earlier, he had been one of only two men, among the ten spies sent to scout out the land, who believed that the Israelites could defeat their enemies and gain the land God had promised them. (See Numbers 13–14.) When the Israelites finally did enter into the promised land, and the land was being distributed, Caleb could have chosen the easy life on the plains, but he chose the heights of the mountains. In addition, he chose the very land of the descendants of Anak, of whom the other ten spies had said, "We seemed like grasshoppers in our own eyes, and we looked the same to them" (Numbers 13:33). For forty years, as the Israelites wandered in the desert, Caleb's spirit of leadership was so strong that he apparently planned to take on the toughest and most fearful adversaries in the land once he had the opportunity.

Here was God's response to Caleb, and I trust that this will be His response to you, as well, as you embrace the truths of true leadership and begin to develop the spirit of leadership in your own life: "Because my servant Caleb has a different spirit and follows me wholeheartedly, I will bring him into the land he went to, and his descendants will inherit it" (Numbers 14:24).

It was Caleb's attitude that made the difference. Will you make it yours, too?

Thought: Leadership is both our past and our destiny. It is the only thing that will fulfill our natural passion for greatness.

Reading: Ephesians 1:11–14

ABOUT THE AUTHOR

D r. Myles Munroe (1954–2014) was an international moti-
vational speaker, best-selling author, educator, leadership mentor,
and consultant for government and business. Traveling extensively
throughout the world, Dr. Munroe addressed critical issues affect-
ing the full range of human, social, and spiritual development.
He was a popular author of more than forty books, including
*The Spirit of Leadership, Becoming a Leader, The Principles and Power
of Vision, The Power of Character in Leadership,* and the devotion-
als *Vision with Purpose and Power, Prayer with Purpose and Power,
A Woman of Purpose and Power,* and *A Man of Purpose and Power.*

Dr. Munroe was the founder and president of Bahamas Faith
Ministries International (BFMI), a multidimensional organiza-
tion headquartered in Nassau, Bahamas. He was the chief exec-
utive officer and chairman of the board of the International Third
World Leaders Association and president of the International
Leadership Training Institute.

Dr. Munroe earned B.A. and M.A. degrees from Oral
Roberts University and the University of Tulsa, and was awarded
a number of honorary doctoral degrees. The parents of two adult
children, Charisa and Chairo (Myles Jr.), Dr. Munroe and his wife,
Ruth, traveled as a team and were involved in teaching seminars
together. Both were leaders who ministered with sensitive hearts
and international vision. In November 2014, they were tragically
killed in an airplane crash en route to an annual leadership conference sponsored by Bahamas Faith Ministries International. A
statement from Dr. Munroe in his book *The Power of Character in
Leadership* summarizes his own legacy: "Remember that character
ensures the longevity of leadership, and men and women of principle will leave important legacies and be remembered by future
generations."